Blackbirds in the Pomegranate Tree

Stories from Ixcotel State Prison

Mary Ellen Sanger

ISBN: 1492957070
ISBN-13: 978-1492957072

For every last one of my vast solidary tribe.

TABLE OF CONTENTS

ACKNOWLEDGMENTS

The women of Ixcotel State Prison gave me these stories. I must first acknowledge the moments we sat knee to knee amidst concrete, concertina wire and questions, looking past it all to seek in each other a tether to something else. Can she fill these moments and keep me from plummeting? Thank you Bertha, Concha, Susa, Natalia, Ana, Citlali, Lucia, Soraya, Flor and the many other women whose presence was every day a guarantee that none of us was truly alone.

My truest fortune was to be the most un-alone of all. I had my fierce, protective herd around me bringing home-baked loaves of bread, chips enough for every woman, water, phone cards, pens and notebooks. I cannot recall their daily visits without feeling to my very marrow the true meaning of "vast." My infinite thanks to those who every day made sure I was connected to someone outside of the walls, who every day whispered my name to someone new who might get me closer to free. To Beth, Gretchen, Cathy, Jim, Jill, Jess, Rebecca, Joanne, Breedlove, Ron, Gustavo, Martha, Maureen (who called every day!), Carlos and Claudia, and of course my entire family of amazing siblings: Cliffie, Dan ("We can get you out of there, Sis!"), Rit, Deb (who unzipped her entire life during those 33 days) and Tes (who learned all about Klonopin). And Bill. Website, reporters, a soothing voice on the phone and all sorts of wisdom and love. Thanks to Russell. Even though. I never expected to have a prison buddy, but couldn't want for a sweeter one than John.

Thanks to editor extraordinaire (and insightful musician/magician) Vanessa Weeks Page for her help with the manuscript, for the group of tremendous Monday evening writers who patiently led me through the first drafts (Caroline, Lauren, Leonard, Melissa, Roderick, Suzanne, Talia and Ziva), and to the Barbara Deming Money for Women Foundation who generously granted me during the early stages. Thanks to The Room of Her Own Foundation who also gave me the gift of creative energy as a finalist for the Gift of Freedom in 2007, when I was flagging in my own belief in my writing. Gail was the first to hear many of these stories as I kept the women close when I first returned to the US. Her friendship is an essential part of me and of this book. Bill again outside... gave me so many ideas he could be co-author. Thanks to Jessica West who is the doubting author's best friend ever. And to Joseph, who has created just the right chemistry of confidence, peace and challenge for me to believe it is time for this book. Now.

AUTHOR'S NOTE

The stories here are real. I have adapted timelines to adjust to the format, and embroidered the women's tales only just a bit, inserting imagination when they recounted pieces of their lives. Of course, their names inside were different.

My own story and the characters in it are based on my truth, my memory and my own perspective at the time. It is the particular oddity of personal narrative, that the story I tell looking out from behind my bars may be different from the one someone else relates looking in. I have been careful to relate facts as clearly I knew them then.

INTRODUCTION

Mary Ellen Sanger is a great writer, there can be no doubt. Her prose goes straight to your very heart and stays there. Beautiful outside and in, Mary Ellen relates the story of her incarceration in Ixcotel prison in Oaxaca, Mexico, and the injustices committed against her; but she does it with such integrity and composure that we almost feel like joining her in her cell. Her tale, as far from sentimentality or self-pity as one could imagine, centers on the other women imprisoned with her, even the "malitas" [bad girls] who get high and hoard their precious stones that, once inhaled, allow them to soar far, far away from the prison.

Mexico is a country where truth is NOT spoken, nor is there a culture of truth. How would the imprisoned women get a chance to speak their own truths? Inside, they tell Mary Ellen of their prodigious life of lies, their prodigious life of truths, they invent a life of dreams and argue that their aspirations remained stuck in the depths of a childhood where remembrance is painful. Mary Ellen listens to them and believes them. Her innocence rescues her cellmates and graces them with a dignity that endears them to us.

To see others with kind eyes is also a way of rescuing oneself.

Mary Ellen puts their stories before hers: Berta, Susa, Natalia, Citlali, Flor, Concha --who stomps a rat to death and once wielded a gun in a bank robbery -- Lucia, Soraya, Ana and all her companions who shared the "talacha" – the relentless sweeping and cleaning of the prison, all her companions who were with her day and night. Mary Ellen sweeps. In prison, as soon as one finishes sweeping it is time to sweep again. They sweep again and again and over and over and at all hours. Everything gets swept. Crimes, shame, anger, sadness all get swept by the brooms.

Mary Ellen's hands blister, but she never shows her wounds. Nor does she show her resulting callouses. She assembles in the courtyard and joins the circle of women who at first reject her for her blond hair and her blue eyes. She shares pistachios with them, and when she innocently tells them that she likes to write poetry but the words won't come here in the pen, Concha sends her a lifeline:

"Don't worry, blondie, someday you'll write the good stuff again."

Their cigarettes are called "Delicados" in cruel irony.

How did Mary Ellen end up in Ixcotel? Simply because in Oaxaca, she attended to an aging North American widower named Russell Ames. Russell and Jean, his piano-playing wife, had bequeathed their extensive local landholdings to the UDLA (University of the Americas, in Mexico City), arranging for the university take possession only after they had both passed away. But when Jean died first, the authorities attempted to remove Russell from his home, from his land. They disregarded the fact that he and Jean had brought much needed improvements to the town -- light and water, a school. They demanded immediate possession of the valuable and storied property. Mary Ellen was a pawn, jailing her was leverage in an attempt to force Russell, a 92-year-old, out of his home.

Mary Ellen had originally come to Mexico to work in tourism and stayed for years and years because she wanted to sit on the steps of our pyramids, swim in the blue-green waters of the Caribbean, traverse the Yucatan peninsula, study the Maya and discover the meaning of their glyphs, read the "Popol Vuh," eat pok-chuc and papadzules. Uxmal, Kabah, Sayil, Xlapak, the ancient world protected by the jungle held no secrets from her. She contemplated the sea from the pyramid in Tulum. In the day, she turned her face to the sun-baked fields; in the night, to the stars.

There are many North Americans who wish to live the "Mexican

Dream," eat a *pitahaya* [dragon fruit] and make themselves a *taco de chapulines* [grasshoppers] and taste *gusanos de maguey* [agave worms]. Mary Ellen, sympathizing with the Zapatista indigenous movement, in 2001 went to Chiapas in support of the communities that the government had destroyed. In La Realidad, in Chenalhó, she sowed and reaped. She sang with the women and children in Las Abejas and helped displaced families. She was moved by the plight of these poorest of Mexicans, the abandoned men, women, elders and children who were never given their place, even though these were the true and original owners of the country. She went into huts and improvised schools and had the children around her drawing, singing, playing, telling their stories. She was able to experience with them, that nothing is more valuable than their own lives and the lives of their ancestors. Jose Santis said to her: "We were once kings."

Mary Ellen's love flows as pure as the rivers in which she bathed.

In the US, Mary Ellen's imprisonment in the Oaxacan jail caused a stir. Senators and Congressmen, friends, acquaintances, tourism agencies pulled together to defend her, turning to the mainstream media: the BBC, NPR, Chicago Tribune, Miami Herald, Los Angeles Times. Her sister and brothers denounced the outrage in their local press and her former schoolmates pitched in to help raise awareness of the situation. Suddenly, Ixcotel became a word in people's mouths.

Behind those bars, a "güerita" [blondie] was struggling for freedom.

Perhaps those who accused her did not realize that they had imprisoned a woman who was so loved. They could not have foretold that her detention would cause such scandal. Nonetheless, the text of Mary Ellen's "Blackbirds in the Pomegranate Tree" does not center on her own desperation, but on the life tales of the incarcerated women who shared their space with her, many of them sentenced to more than fifteen years in prison. Mary Ellen, in addition to portraying how our lives can change in an instant, shows us through her writing, that to take "others" into account is not so difficult. The only thing one must do is to step outside of oneself.

Nobody (in the US or Mexico) understood that in Ixcotel, Mary Ellen lived in a cell stacked with women, or that she swept and mopped the jail floor every morning along with the other women who called her "gringuita." In an expression of solidarity with the women, Mary Ellen earned their trust and affection because she dived right into the "talacha" [sweeping chores], she never complained and did not squirm from the primitive latrines with their buckets of water. She shared her soap and her towel, the sweets that were brought in by friends, and took deliberate steps to avoid becoming depressed. Alongside the other women, she stood in long lines for the telephone. More than anything else, it was caring about "the others" that helped keep her spirit intact -- defending the gullible from corrupt lawyers, being a careful listener, caring for their self-esteem. In this way she helped herself as well as her fellow inmates, who often tended toward defeat, abandoning their own cause in the face of insurmountable hurdles and grim realities.

"Blackbirds in the Pomegranate Tree" is a life lesson. If they were to throw me in jail, I would carry it with me to read each night, as some read the Bible or the Gospels. In its pages I would find strength and faith in humankind, and I would know that to believe in "the others" is a path to salvation.

I suppose and believe that I am not wrong in saying that for Mary Ellen, Mexico is a woman who one day, will find herself.

Elena Poniatowska

October 2013

Translated with the generous assistance of Sandra Tapia and Bill Fuchs

KEEPING TIME TO EARTH

From Uruapan to Nuevo San Juan Parangaricútiro

At the top of a small rise, giant ferns laced the park in watercolor light, steamy primeval green. Doña Jacinta sold us plump cobs of steaming sapphire corn from a deep basket covered with an oversized napkin ticked with pink and green embroidered strawberries. We sat on stumps and talked with her while we ate the earthy, hard-kernelled maize, sparkled with lime juice. She had not known that blue eyes could speak Spanish, she said. We asked her about the church in Nuevo San Juan Pa-ran-ga-ri-cú-ti-ro, parsing out the name in pronounceable syllables. "It's a nice walk, just over the hill from Uruapan," she said, and wrapped an extra cob for each of us, wiping her hands on a red plaid apron and wishing us well in her native Purépecha.

It didn't sink in that she might have been provisioning us for a trek until we were well along the remote, sun-scorched path around the base of a mountain. We walked for six miles on un-weathered volcanic rock, jagged as a broken heart. The dry grate of the hardened lava complained underfoot, as if it were still unaccustomed to its solid form. This volatile heart of Mexico spit out over the countryside only decades ago by Paricutín volcano, swallowed a whole town and now cut through the soles of my espadrilles. In fairness, doña Jacinta had said the walk was "nice"—not "easy." Fields of birds of paradise skewered the cloudless blue with their vivid orange beaks, and we reached out to a horse grazing shoulder-high in grass, to stroke his chocolate flank. Purple passionflower vines wound through the brush perfuming the path, and the bracing mountain panorama would have had us whirling in pure enchantment, were it not for fear of losing our balance on the shifting rocks underfoot.

When we arrived in Nuevo San Juan Parangaricútiro, my soles were flopping, and I entered town with a thwap thwap that turned heads. The church was easy to find, its two bell towers casting long shadows over a lively plaza where children kicked a split orange and graying men sold ice pops of guanábana, sapote and mango. Inside the church was cool and quiet. We took seats in the back pew and watched as the faithful approached the altar—dancing. Two steps forward, one step back. Everyone who enters knows the steps. Two steps forward, one back, a sway in the hips and shoulders. Doña Jacinta told us that the dance began in 1944 when the original San Juan was destroyed in a sudden hot lava rage with the eruption of Paricutín volcano. She said the congregants dance now to remind God that they are ready—that with this dance they can keep time to the shuddering earth. Tomorrow will be just as unknown as today, and the people of San Juan Parangaricútiro will be ready. Even the children danced to the altar that day, to no accompaniment other than a flutter of sparrows in the rafters.

I had my doubts about doña Jacinta's version of history, but I liked its kinetic nature. Seismic, explosive Mexico is accustomed to colliding with herself. This is why I fell in love with her. She matched my insides. Mexicans live in a land that has never been at rest in her skin, a land where friction and upheaval are commonplace, and they have adapted. In Mexico the earth is not quiet, and in the seventeen years I lived and listened there, I perfected my own wobbly equilibrium, learning the dance, learning to live and love with some clear certainty that everything will change tomorrow. Two steps forward, one step back.

THE SNAP OF THE LOCK

From Holding to the Women's Compound

Two guards armed with clubs led me through a concrete corridor following a delicate ribbon of sun, hashed by the shadow of crossed wire overhead. Along the edges men chattered, seated on concrete blocks or on the ground in informal groups. They hand-twisted copper wire into bicycle shapes. Some painted sailing ships on old light bulbs. Others drew long, curved needles through tough leather hides to make soccer balls.

"*Oye, una gringa!*"

"Put that one aside for me, man!"

"Look at that! A sweet new face, *compadres!*"

They pursed their lips and whistled, blew kisses. I didn't feel threatened—I had two hulking male guards with me—but I knew the numbers: 110 women, 1500 men and one and only one *gringa*. I would stare, too, if I were fighting the boredom of their gray walls. Concrete floors, black uniforms, and suddenly one pale-skinned sun-streaked blonde.

The guards escorted me to the women's compound, their heavy boots careful to match the pace of my sandals. They didn't rush me.

"We're almost there."

"The women inmates have sewing classes. Art. Typing. You'll have lots to do."

Welcome to Ixcotel Penitentiary.

Their black heels in steady cadence, a club swaying at the hip – now they were the authority I would have to obey. I hadn't had much experience with authority other than my own inner voice, which often whispered. If I ignored my own whispers, I might end up discontent or caught in the rain with no umbrella. Now there was a club to factor into the equation. To the guards, we walked toward the beginning. To me, the end. My sandals dragged along the last few meters before the gated entrance to the women's compound, prolonging what was left of not being in there, with them.

The boss lady met me at the entrance. Once the guards passed me off, they pushed the heavy door closed behind us. It vibrated for far too long after the snap of the lock—a hum of metal on metal that intensified as I entered the buzz of the compound, where no one was sitting still, no one was quiet. The boss lady, fiftyish, wore a short belted dress checkered in blues and red. Her duo-tone ponytail, dark roots with bottle-blonde, was gathered tight at the top of her head like a fountain. She had penciled a warning in the severe black arch of her brows. "Don't mess with me."

"Check in with the receiving guard and I'll be back when she's done with you."

Done with me.

It wasn't like drowning; I could still hear. Screams bounced off two-story concrete block walls. It wasn't like suffocation; I could still smell. Cigarette smoke clung to a wave of rancid oil from the kitchen. It wasn't like being hit by a train or falling into a crevasse, my feet stepped square on the ground. Not a heart attack. Not a black hole. It was jail-prison-penitentiary-*la cárcel*. It was injustice-unknown-freedom erased. It was all of these things. It was all I had at that instant and it was nothing. A sudden loss, a darkening, a plummet.

I could see only what was directly in front of me. Though I could choose very little now, I chose not to see wide-angle panoramas. I chose not to see the threat of a fourteen-year sentence. I chose not to take in the entirety of the compound that seemed at once impossibly small and impossibly complex, the universe just after the big bang. I chose, in that moment, not to register the urgent voices of the women inside. I could barely hear my own voice, wispy, suddenly timorous. I couldn't tell how I felt anymore, here in the dark bright sun of my new home. I chose to pinpoint my gaze on what was in front of me, and shaded my eyes from the glare and heat, swallowing hard.

I stopped in front of a sloped desk with my arms wrapped around the yoga mat and blanket a friend had given me to for bedding, a black plastic garbage bag with clothes at my feet. Only thirty seconds into my first day in the Ixcotel women's compound, I saw threats in eyebrows, in words, in the insistence of the iron door that would keep me in.

The stocky guard in black uniform tee-shirt cleaned her fingers on the Arts and Culture page of *El Imparcial,* covered her chicken and green rice with it, and clicked her pen.

"You speak Spanish?"

"*Sí.*"

She wrote "110" on a piece of scrap paper.

"There are 110 women inside, and they'll be watching you. All of them. More than I will. Don't leave your property unattended—not a pen, not a bar of soap—because when you come back looking for your soap, *mujer,* it won't be around. And nobody took it."

She drew a zero with a piercing line through it.

I nodded. "Okay. *Sí.*"

I squeezed my blanket, feeling ridiculous and scared, a child hugging a stuffed bear as the teacher reads the playground rules on the opening day of kindergarten.

"If you can, send your clothes out for your friends to wash. Right now it's brassieres. Five or six have disappeared in the last few days. And nobody took them."

She engraved two bold parallel lines on the remaining empty space on her scrap, with too much emphasis for a doodle. Bra-less clotheslines. Bars. Train tracks out.

"Inside, nobody knows what you did, nobody cares. Listen to the boss lady. And stay out of trouble. Don't show up late for roll call. We all try to stay pretty happy in here." She crumpled the note.

"Okay."

"You get me?"

"*Sí.*"

Three minutes into this first day in the women's compound at Ixcotel, and I was already lying to protect myself. I hadn't "gotten" much during the past six days since my arrest.

"Okay, I'm done with you."

Done with me.

The boss lady returned, smoothed the stray hairs around the dark roots of her ponytail, and spoke to me in passable English.

"They call me Chofis. Given name's Sofia. I'll clear a space on the shelves for your things later—here, throw your bedding in with the rest—I'll present you to the ladies."

Meet the ladies

Watch my pens.

Stay happy.

Get it.

I threw my bedding in with the rest.

Ixcotel. At least it has a tantalizing name.

BEFORE THE WINDS ERASE THEM

From San Diego to Mérida and back

One year out of college in 1980, I moved from upstate New York to San Diego, California. I trekked across country with a friend, lugging a warning from my mom that California was plagued by terrible things like mudslides, brush fires, earthquakes and orgies in hot tubs with lime jello. She kissed me goodbye and told me to practice safe sex, knowing that if she tried to keep her curious daughter any closer she would only be further away.

I wanted to continue the career in scholarly publishing I had started after college, though a purely career-oriented move would have sent me to New York City or Boston. Following my inner whisper, I opted instead for adventure on the west coast, as I daydreamed romantic images of white sailboats against the San Diego skyline. Shortly after my arrival there, a major international publisher moved in from New York, a highly unusual move in the publishing industry at that time, and one I took as an omen. Harcourt Brace Jovanovich hired me as a Production Editor for academic journals with ear-bending titles like Biochemical and Biophysical Research Communications, Journal of Differential Equations and Archives of Colloid and Interface Science. Before the dawn of the computer age, we kept elaborate records in #2 pencil, nudging a manuscript through its paces with artists, copyeditors, proofreaders and printers. I loved the business, loved working in an office of young, inventive book people, and after six years, at 28 years old, I was a manager with a foothold on the corporate ladder, doing what young career people do.

I lived in an apartment complex with a pool on the patio. I supported the San Diego Zoo and local theater. I happy-houred at smart bars on Fridays and tequila-ed at seaside parties on weekends. I had a boyfriend who raised Persian cats and sent bouquets of freesias and tulips to my office, another who baked plum pies from scratch and could tie cherry stems into knots with his tongue. Neither spoke Spanish and neither understood why I traveled hours to Baja California in Mexico every few months on a red trolley and a bus with no shocks, to buy a few cassette tapes of Silvio Rodriguez' music.

"Mom, I can't marry a man who thinks the sun is a planet!"

"So don't talk about the solar system with him."

"Maybe I'll just take off for Mexico."

"That's my smart daughter. Mexicans think the sun is a god!"

"It's not?"

"Follow your heart, honey."

From a few rungs up on the corporate ladder, I realized that I wanted more fluidity, more freedom. On their ladder, I would have to hang on with both hands tight, both feet firmly planted in their world. While my friends laminated their business cards, proud of their new titles, I backed down from promotions that required a compromise of my budding professional morality. With too much belief in curves, I wasn't learning the rigid, angled rules of engagement in an aggressively controlled corporate world.

"Do you know what the most important part of publishing *is*?" my boss asked, cornering me with a question impossible to answer.

"Making the paper?" She didn't appreciate my irony. We had different perspectives. If she defined success for me, I was doomed.

After six years in San Diego, the only mystery my future held was the increasingly annoying question of why I didn't fit. Mexico fluttered just over the border, waving devilishly vibrant ribbons of melon and fuchsia that I could not ignore. I sat in the public library after work to read books on Mayan studies and the Yucatan Peninsula. Voluptuous glyphs slithered across the pages. *Balam*, a plump spotted jaguar. *Chaak*. A curly-nosed storm god. I read rain-soaked creation myths in the *Popol Vuh* and listened to music played on ancient reed flutes and shells. I experimented on friends with recipes for *Pok Chuk* and *Papadzules*, and memorized the grid of streets that transected the Yucatecan capital. Though I had never been in Merida, by the time I boarded the plane, I felt I was headed home.

In Merida, I took a leave of absence from my publishing job for half a year—to think. I walked down any crooked cobbled paths that held promise, and to me, they all did. I appeared in tourists' photos of Mayan temples, as I wrote for hours atop the Governor's Palace at Uxmal or the Temple of the Warriors at Chichén Itzá. I lived my seductive glyphic dream for six full and free months.

Musky scents of moss and bat manure inside the pyramids intoxicated me. Blowing the dust off my college majors of Spanish and Anthropology, I scrambled through ruins with tantalizing names: Uxmal, Labná, Kabah, Sayil, Xlapak; ancient worlds sheathed by jungle, holding hard to their secrets. Centuries ago, Mayans invented zero and calculated the movement of the heavens. Now, their perfect mathematics tripped me as I stumbled over crumbling walls and fallen capstones. From the top of a pyramid, I lifted my arms straight to my sides and the sun threw my serpentine shadow down the steep steps. I was a sundial. My left arm shadowed wide over the pre-Colombian past; my hand cradled a bas-relief turtle. My right arm held a Canon camera, a pendulum into the present, swinging from my wrist. My body was long as a river. The flow of then and now threw me off balance. Spanish has a perfect word for this disconcerting perception: *vaivén,* the dizziness of going and coming.

I met a man with access to the ruins, and returned to the pyramids at midnight. Yes, it was a clear night of full moon. The graceful curved architecture of the Pyramid of the Magician was never stonier and more silent. The imposing structure, steps rising at an unusually steep 60° angle, grew tall and taller still until the moon was a pearl, studded atop the uppermost temple. Archaeologists study the five phases of the pyramid's construction over a period of four centuries during the Classic Maya period. Folklorists compile versions of the "Magician" story, which circle around a magical egg that hatched a dwarf who built the pyramid in a day. I had done my reading. That night, as rivulets of reflected light trickled down the steps and pooled at the base, I plugged into this version of the world that honored the imagination and accomplishment of ancients, that permitted uncommon beauty in light and silence, that allowed mystery to rush the beat of a heart.

The next morning, I sat on the pyramid steps, now drying from the moon-shower that had swept over us the night before. Eagles inscribed soaring signatures into a sky that smelled of wood fires and mildewed antiquity. I ran my fingers over monuments carved with whispering stone turtles, bats, skulls and quetzal birds. Around me, furrowed fields baked by a dagger-rayed Mayan sun covered centuries of tangled corn roots, minerals from the sweat of ox and plowman, bodies of decaying insects and ancient tributes on bits of broken pottery. It was almost time to leave and I felt it in my fingertips and the soles of my feet.

There was an elder in the town of Muna who kept tiny figurines and pottery vessels whole and in shards, in crumpled paper bags, catalogued and tucked into drawers and cupboards in his bright blue and yellow house. He had been walking for nearly eighty years in Muna, picking up what he found, tucking pieces away in bags. He showed me a letter from a prominent Mayanist at Yale University who complimented his very thorough collection. Don Gregorio had blue eyes, and told me that the earth in his town held secrets. I hadn't walked on secret-specked earth before I met Mexico. I felt a prickle in my toes.

"What secrets, don Gregorio?"

"Those who walked here before us didn't control what you and I think we control. No umbrellas, no nightly news, no pills. The ancestors expected nothing. Their only certainty was that tomorrow would be surprising."

"And these secrets you talk about, don Gregorio?"

He reached into a crumpled paper bag labeled A-145 and held a perfect pottery bowl in his hand, with a faint blue painted rim.

"Like our eyes," he said.

Handing it toward me, he pretended to fumble, and we laughed. Holding it close I could make out elaborate painted figures with headdresses and earplugs. They seemed to be lost in discussion, fat glyphs like embryos curled around each other in the space between them, caught in a moment of silent mitosis.

"Their words are secret. Their purpose is secret. Maybe we can learn the date, guess at the words, but the real message is gone. It wasn't meant to be this way. Someone painstakingly painted these certain words on this bright bowl so that everyone would know."

He took my hand and continued.

"You thought I had answers, didn't you?"

We smiled deep blue and he pressed my hand to his heart.

"Make your words count now, before the winds erase them," he said. "Tomorrow they will be difficult to decode. It's not an answer, it's just a suggestion from an old man."

Returning to San Diego, I felt triumphant for having lived my Mexican dream, rich and intricate, mysterious and challenging. Much too soon after returning, I began to trip over new subtitles inserted in the frames of my home story. I felt suddenly emptier in southern California, where context strongly advised that happiness was the newest car, the cutest boyfriend, the sleekest designer wardrobe and the longest waiting list for a friend to catch you available for dinner. I heard the *palomas* of Mexico's tranquil plazas *purrt-purrt* in my head. I closed my eyes to return to a shaded afternoon in the giant embrace of almond trees. A vendor sells chile-sparked jicama and papaya from the edge of a fountain where kids, lively as puppies, throw shiny centavos into the sun-washed water. I hurried in my memory, back to that place where I didn't hurry anywhere. A dark woman in white embroidered dress walks with astonishing grace over uneven sidewalks with a basket of *pitahayas* posed atop her head. A Zen-centered Carmen Miranda, she has a magnetic connection to the earth. I envy her. And the mystery? Where was the mystery? The Yucatan teased with a strum of guitar and a whiff of the market's vibrancy, the perfume of blackened roast corn over glowing coals. My young professional niche in San Diego became a cage. There was no getting rid of Mexico.

I QUIT

From San Diego to Cancún

Don Gregorio's words wound around my memories of Mexico, clear and concise. "Make your words count." So with two painstakingly chosen words I quit my job, and looked for a new career that would take me back to Mexico. I couldn't put blinders on and not see her. I couldn't un-smell her or reel in again the curiosity that she had uncoiled. I couldn't find an octagonal hole in San Diego where the Mexicanized-me would fit. It was clear that I must return. I was miserable without Mexico. Though friends called me "brave" to make a radical change when my life appeared to be in order, valor played little part in my decision—nor did any appreciation of order. I was greedy. I simply wanted more of what I wanted. I wanted to be in that place where my senses and tenses ignited. Mine was a lust for place that overshadowed any sense of order or purpose.

A friend who worked in the travel business told me about a large, prestigious tour operator in Chicago, known as *número uno* for promoting Mexico. They needed Mexico-based representatives. Not much in my paper-focused professional background recommended me for a job in people-oriented tourism, but I would get this job, there was no question. I trusted that my desire alone would be enough. I swallowed my fear of public speaking and presented my version of a capable, confident vacation professional in front of six evaluators with intimidating stares, and after three cross-country interviews I was heading to Cancún with a job as "Mobile Resort Representative." Cancún was only a few hours away from Chichén

Itzá, where I had first dizzied at the cool stony secrets of the pyramids.

A fair-skinned, fair-eyed blonde who kept to the shade and wore high SPF before it became recommendable, I didn't much care about the beach. I didn't care particularly about tourism, either. I wanted the job so that I could be in Mexico. The Caribbean breezes were only a perk. But when I arrived in Cancun in the fall of 1987, I took to this work of tourism and it to me. It allowed for more curves.

My fear of public speaking gone, I was suddenly on stage and playing with groups of hundreds of new tourists.

"Spanish is easy. You see the shops, you know what you're getting. Chocolatería?"

"Chocolate!" they yell from the crowd, primed with free drinks.

"Licorería?"

"Liquor!"

"Tortillería?"

"Tortillas!"

And the crowd is giggling and feeling proud of themselves when I give them:

"Ferretería?"

And the giggles turn to laughter as they yell out "Ferrets!"

"Sorry guys. Just like in English – you buy heads at a Head Shop? There ARE some exceptions to the rule. A ferretería is actually a hardware store. You get your ferrets at a *tienda de mascotas*. But why don't you wait till you get back home to buy your ferret anyway. They don't like the sun."

I feel the goofy effects of their margaritas, and I'm on my way with my new career introducing people to the Mexico that I love.

IN PERFECT GEOMETRY

From Cancún to Huatulco

Mobile Resort Reps had a short professional shelf life. We were "on" six days a week, long hours if planes were delayed, and after the partying, free trips to Jamaica and a few steamy romances, most lasted a year, maybe two, and left tanned and weary. But I already had one career in publishing, and professional momentum and a growing interest in the field led me headlong into this second career in tourism. After my first year, I begged off the "meet and greet" for more challenging work to develop a new resort opening on the coast of Oaxaca. We were to bring the first charter planes into the resort.

"Where in the world is Watusi?" my mother asked.

"Huatulco. It's in the state of Oaxaca. Wa-TUL-Ko, Wa-HA-Ka." I sounded it out phonetically.

"Sounds like a snort and a sneeze."

"It's supposed to be rugged and beautiful."

"Death Valley is rugged and beautiful. Sometimes it's dangerous when those two mix. Be careful. Wear your sunscreen."

"I know, Mom. I love you, too."

Now a "Resort Manager," I had a briefcase, a uniform and a schedule for a winter full of Saturday night planes. I dived into Huatulco, as much as a tourism professional who wore a knee-length polyester skirt, sensible pumps and a blouse with a regulation-tied scarf could dive.

The international airport in Huatulco was a tiny thatched-roofed palapa terminal. Mariachis played on the tarmac after the first plane landed. The hotels planned Italian Night buffets and volleyball matches on the beach. The guides, unaccustomed to international tourism, quickly learned enough English to make a mid-westerner feel at home, with terms like "Cheese head" and "Chicago Bears." I did my professional duty to see that 150 passengers a week filled their vacation time with as much relaxing Huatulco as they could stand, with reminders to wear sunscreen, as we were closer to god there.

My most vivid memories are not of the sun.

In the Lagunas de Manialtepec, herons and egrets hide tall and lean amidst the mangroves. At night the silent lake glows from within. The oars of our boat trail soft green ribbons, curls of phosphorescent lake-whispers.

Pale lizards in the bedroom make kissing sounds in the dark.

In sheer moonlight thrown about the boulders of the beach like a shawl, a sea turtle waltzes at the fringe of the sea carving quarter-notes in the sand. Frilled by curls of kelp her diamond-studded carapace sways with the rare grace of a leviathan and on this night she intones future, in slow-motion carving a chalice in the sand to receive her round, pliant eggs. Then, in perfect geometry, she returns to the sea at precisely the spot where she first met the moon, now swallowed by the Pacific, no trace of her midnight dance, except for the steady beat of two hundred new and urgent songs.

Myth holds that a massive indestructible cross was erected on the beach in Huatulco by Quetzalcoatl, the Plumed Serpent. Presiding there for centuries, it resisted lightning and the greed of pirates—until the devout hacked slivers of it to hold in their hands, bit by bit reducing the great cross to a cane that toppled in an ocean gale.

By a bonfire to celebrate the cross that resisted everything but faith, I eat iguana bathed in *chile pasilla*—assuring, friends said, that I will return.

The air in Huatulco was dry and briny, the hills around us spiked with bare trees and brush. My local friends had skin the color of the earth that cradled cactus roots. I worked six days a week in luxury hotels and spent the seventh eating fried grasshoppers and holding dark-haired babies over the baptismal font. I learned songs in Zapotec and patted corn *masa* into wannabe circular tortillas. I burrowed into Mexico.

I was where I wanted to be, and responsible for making lots of people really, really happy. Vacationers could be a cheerful bunch if their trip went as planned. If a plane cancelled or luggage disappeared, the training I received in tourism diplomacy gave me the tools to aim for poised control. "Just be present." Our client service approach had a Buddhist-like mantra that calmed me while I tried in turn to calm tourists. Friends from home had subtitled my name-badge: Mary Ellen Sanger, P.P.P. – Professionally Pleasant Person. I learned the business in exciting chapters, from aviation to international relations, as I ran in my polyester skirt and low-heeled pumps from the airport control tower to the town mayor's office in support of the growth of the tourism. Tourism had officially become my career.

ONE EARTHLY THING

From Huatulco to Cabo San Lucas

After Huatulco I was no longer a novice. I moved from one new resort to another to set up programs, train new staff, establish procedures and to be the corporate face of the agency for local politicians, hotel managers and airport directors. After two years, I was an old-timer. I lived in a luxury hotel with daily housekeeping service and a bellman who knew what time I returned at night. I cooked black beans on a hot plate in a marbled bathroom, and had to sneak overnight visitors in through the sliding patio doors beachside. I was in Mexico. But I dreamed of having a broom of my own, in a corner of my own, in a place where I could pound a nail in the wall to hang my Huichol yarn drawing, tend a plot of zinnias, and prepare *pipián* with pumpkin seeds on an honest-to-goodness stove. Sometimes life throws you just what you want.

Angel and I moved into a thatched roof brick home with open arched windows —no glass—in rustic and romantic Cabo San Lucas where I was assigned to develop the new charter program for the company. We had two cats and a yard with *damiana, toloache, verdolagas* and coreopsis. A hollow-toned bell on a bull skull hung in the middle of our splintery wooden gate. We could see the ocean from our home and hear sea lions on the rocks by the famed Cabo arch when the wind blew right. Each year, the same hummingbird with a red dot at her throat returned and knocked her delicate beak against our wooden door. "I am here." Moonflowers bloomed in the night with a startling perfume, and the sheer bulk of afternoon rainbows threatened to topple in mosaic stripes onto the desert floor. I awakened to nature, love and intimacy. Face to face with an electric-eyed wildcat. Sixteen limbs tangled in the same bed at night if both cats joined us. Meteor showers where we spun like dervishes, arms raised to catch the melting stars in our hands.

Then the seasons shifted and the winter planeloads demanded I return to the nomadic life—again to Cancún. Cancún is the landing spot for anyone who works upward in the tourism scene in Mexico—and every time I landed I requested out on the next plane. Cancún's gloss was not for me. This time, with my life in Cabo San Lucas rooted and full of discovery, I had all I needed, so I did what I had learned to do. I took the alternative path, the one my whispering heart instructed, and I quit. I left the agency to stay in Cabo, and stay with love. I was hired as the Groups and Conventions Manager of a 300-room luxury hotel and fell into it like family, having already worked with the hotel on the other side of the counter.

Several seasons of harvesting bowls full of cactus fruit passed. Angel and I grew closer through disastrous floods that melted the roadways, weeks without running water, living with scorpions the size of lobsters and with enormous black night-moths that clung like bad omens to the mosquito netting around our bed. It wasn't a luxurious existence, but it was ours—rugged and beautiful like a raw diamond. The love and intimacy that had enraptured me were still lovely and intimate on good days, on bad days soured by Angel's empty bottles and notes on our refrigerator chalkboard with a rarely-fulfilled promise: "Gone into town for just one beer. Be back soon." We kept a magnet on the fridge with a motto from Rainer Maria Rilke: "One earthly thing truly experienced, even once, is enough for a lifetime."

The palm fronds of our roof kept the floor of our home dry through the rage of tropical storms. Yet every afternoon, a quarter-sized dollop of sunlight streamed through the leaves onto the brick of my kitchen floor. I could see no gap in the weave that permitted this puddle of light to drip where rain had not. I interrupted the beam and caught the light in the palm of my hand. It felt dangerous, as if I could hurtle it against the wall and it would become shards. It felt potent, as if it could dance up my arm and plant seed sparks in my heart. I closed my fist around this one spot of sun that quite by accident fell upon my kitchen floor, upon my palm, and tucked it into my pocket – hoping to harness the liquidity of photons that can make it through anything.

One morning the desk clerk at the hotel handed me a message as I arrived at work.

"You got a phone call."

The number was my mother's—she never called me long distance. I feared something had happened to my sister. When I dialed and my sister picked up, I felt a whoosh of relief.

"Mom died."

"How?"

"In her sleep. Can't you just see? She walked to her window last night and wished on the same six stars she did every night, and decided it was time."

I remember my mom picking raspberries in summer. She pushed through the sea of canes with a pail, defying the plump, furry bumblebees and insistent thorns. We never understood why she seemed to enjoy that harvest that came with risk of stings and scrapes. She said that to pick raspberries right, you had to know when it was time. The raspberry falls, sweet into her palm, with just a slight tug when it has had its fill of sun and grace.

I called Angel and told him about my Mom and that I would work the full day, but please come to pick me up at five. Five o'clock, five thirty, five forty, five fifty, six fifteen… and Angel showed up drunk. He drove home because I couldn't see through my tears.

"You knew I needed you today."

"You don't understand, Mari—I would be this way if it were my own mother."

I decided it was time. After four earnest years, I let go.

Even jades fracture; even gold ruptures, even quetzal plumes tear:

Not forever on earth: only a brief time here!

Nezahualcoyotl, 1470

NOWHERE NEAR

From Cabo San Lucas to Cancún

In 1995 I left Cabo's doubloon desert moons and new-penny dawns to return again to Cancún. Alone and nearing forty, I had earned thin pesos through years of severe devaluations. Good money was a good idea. I returned to the company that hired me all those years ago, to co-manage the local agency they had established, in one of the highest profile jobs in the company, one of the most respected jobs in the city, and a staff of 200 who looked to me for leadership. I knew from the beginning that it would be a challenge to adapt again, to this Cancún that seemed to have become a necessary evil.

In the humid, tropical breath of the Mexican Caribbean, the clouds do not float distinct and independent as in the mountainous desert. In the *Caribe* they wilt at the edges, melt into the enormous expanse of sky that weights the sea in place. The clouds hang low and sigh, exhausted from the heat. This was my fourth assignment in Cancún.

In the *Caribe* the birds pierce through the muggy air with loud cries, long, thin and uplifted like the palm leaves that hide them. They question. A breeze leads the ocean into my lungs, where it settles with the scents of moist leaves and damp lime. Maybe it won't be so bad. I know people in Cancún. I have friends that I love as family after eight years of coming and going. Cancún has grown but vendors still wheel water through her streets and yell "*Aguaaaaaa!*" Mexico still pokes through the paved-over jungle.

A great asteroid fell in these parts, in Chicxulub, and caused the demise of the dinosaurs, flattening the countryside forever: the highest point in the entire peninsula is the Hyatt Regency. But Cancún held mountains of memories, and for a time I felt comfortable climbing, and digging in with new gardens, a new love, new challenges.

Then my Mexico disappeared into the foam parties and wet T-shirts of Spring Break.

At the *Bladder Buster Beach Bash*, students gathered to drink at 10am. Their provocatively nuanced slogans on not-yet-tanned bodies set the tone for their vacation.

"Do It While Your Daddy's Not Looking"

"I Had Twenty Before Noon"

"Not Yet Wet"

The busboys who refilled vats of salsa and endless bowls of chips tried to read the tease of chests around them to practice their English.

"*No sé.* It's something about her father."

Our numbers were good that year, a 20% increase over the previous year. Thousands of eager college students arrived on planes from Philadelphia, New York, Chicago. While I monitored sales for the agency, I wondered if any of these students had considered spending their break in the south helping a less-fortunate family build a new home, or working to reduce youth violence in urban Detroit.

By the crystalline "too-blue-to-be-true" waters of the Caribbean the students danced over powdery sands, reggae booming in the loudspeakers. The kids grasped twelve-ounce plastic cups with lathered beers, one in each hand—because at this party, as long as nobody peed, beers were free—hence the nifty alliterative "Bladder Buster" party banner. The sentry, cool as a Mayan stone warrior, stationed himself at the bathrooms to ensure that no one entered. A rope across a great expanse of sweetly cool sand prevented the kids from pee-ing in the ocean. Cancún's sand is unique in Mexico for its composition of limestone that doesn't hold heat like silica sand—the remains of ancient shells pulverized by eons of ocean provided "air-conditioned" sand for always-comfortable beach walks. The Spring Breakers were oblivious to the history that collected between their toes. After free beers, they were oblivious to a lot.

To keep students in line at the hotels, our representatives in bright floral shirts and navy blue shorts politely advised the kids that the credit card number they left at the front desk would be charged in the event of setting mattresses on fire or throwing up into the lampshades. Our reps helped find the purse left in a taxi after the Purdue freshman returned from Senor Frogs weaving like a fumigated spider. They sold Pub Crawls, Caribbean Carnivals, Coco Bongo Nites, Pirate's Adventures, Mango Tango Fests and a very occasional trip to the ruins. With free beer on the return bus.

At the top rung of the ladder in this career, I had hit bottom hard.

This was not the sensual, mysterious Mexico I had fallen hard for a decade-plus ago.

The sun had relinquished its poetry to dollar signs. By professional necessity, I now defined a trip to the ruins in terms of busload factors. I was writing the same disciplinary actions, sifting through the same financial reports, and responding to the same corporate pressures I had so purposefully left behind in San Diego.

I had lost my perspective. I started out professionally stimulated by growing within this "clean" industry that introduced Mexico to hard-working vacationers, who might not have discovered a world outside of Milwaukee or Pittsburgh, who might not have ever seen a crocodile or a spider monkey, who might not have heard the echoes in the pyramids or seen the humble reed homes along the road, where Mexicans without sombreros and sarapes watched

"Dallas" on television. They might not have had a chance to appreciate similarities and differences. Their worlds might not be as large or as small.

Now I saw them arriving on chartered planes to spend three days in an all-inclusive resort. They complained about the view from their hotel room, even though they spent so little time there because the pool bar served icy fruit drinks with tequila and the bartender remembered their names. Nighttime brought contests—a couple could win a bottle of Kahlua if she could pass an egg from inside one leg of his shorts to the other, using only her mouth. Guests rarely set their tan and sandaled feet off the lush grounds of the hotel, dotted with palms imported from Veracruz and peacocks native to nowhere near Mexico. They returned to tell their friends how much they loved Mexico and couldn't wait to get back.

No, I love Mexico! I want to get back!

I pulled at a loose thread that hung in the corner of my memory, to unravel another decision. Hadn't I learned this once or twice already?

Follow your heart.

In 1998 I started taking writing retreats to escape from Cancún and get closer to the lyrical Mexico I had come to love. Every six months, a poet from California gathered writers in the tiny village of San Pablo Etla outside of the capital of Oaxaca. Donna's writing sessions helped to open the creative part of me that the demands of my job had crowded out. A month before Spring Break of 1999, I vacationed in Oaxaca for the third time to write. There, I met Meg, an 83-year-old Quaker woman and yoga practitioner. We had a conversation under the bougainvillea at the rustic Bed and Breakfast where the group stayed.

"But I am at the top of the professional pyramid in tourism."

"And?"

"And any other job would be a step down."

"How?"

"Less responsibility, less pay."

"Do you need to feel so responsible?"

"Not really—I imagine I would be happier selling flowers in a market in Guanajuato."

"Do you need a lot of money?"

"Well, no...I've never had a lot of money, and I've been fine."

"So?"

I had tea that night with a writer from New York. Bill gave me a thousand ideas about where I could publish, if I only had time to write. I made a plan.

I quit!

It took a year and a half to untangle from the responsibility of the job, but in mid-2000 I left Cancún for rural Oaxaca, to volunteer and to write.

Shocked at the announcement, my friends prodded.

"What will you *do* in Oaxaca? I mean, in Cancún everybody knows you, you have a great job, you are busy all the time!"

"Yeah, that's it. I have no time for me. I will write. Volunteer. Do what I want."

"You'll be back before you know it. You love it here."

I had perfected the tourism smile. People thought I loved Cancún. I wore my badge well: No Bad News. No Rain. And if it does rain, look for the rainbow. Green-blue-indigo-violet. Potholes? Unrest?

With the advent of the Internet, I had new access to online literature and the themes of marginalization, militarization, globalization and polarization started to poke holes into the irreality of my touristic Mexico. Could tourism bring worlds together? It was no longer clear to me. I read about the Seattle protests against the World Trade Organization, and the anti-globalization/pro-indigenous movement under my own roof, the Zapatistas. I learned an activist's alphabet. NAFTA, WTO, FTAA, PPP, IMF, WB, and EZLN. I knew I needed to draw closer to the "other" Mexico, the one I identified with—the questioning, curious, struggling one, not the Mexico dolled up for tourists. I was adding lust for purpose to my lust for place.

AS YOU CATCH YOUR BREATH

From Cancún to Oaxaca

Oaxaca is an area of striking iridescence and visibly rooted culture, one of the most indigenous states in the republic, and also among the poorest. I arrived a week after a strong earthquake shook the city. Downtown, rubble from ancient buildings lined the edges of cobbled streets. Banners throughout the city solicited solidarity for residents whose roofs did not withstand the jolt. In the quiet village of San Pablo Etla where I had chosen to live, at the foot of the mountains the dry corn stalks swayed in rutted fields, and stout concrete-block homes stood unmoved. Locals told me that the only indication of the tremor was the coffee that sloshed out of the pot over the morning fire, spotting the earthen floor. The mountains buried tectonic slips further below the surface. In the mountains, they merely nod and say "Again."

I chose Oaxaca with my six senses. It was like coming home—I had eaten the iguana. I quickly found a niche to do more of what I wanted to do. I participated in a rural community. I wrote, I lent a hand, drew close to children and elders and animals and plants. I walked over mountain paths in the tag-along light of the pre-dawn moon, listening to the sunrise as chirring insects hid away, and the first birds awakened. I shifted under my skin. Oaxaca glistened with rare ambers, jades, and rubies. Indigenous colors. A scarlet bird on a golden cactus bloom. A serpent carved from soft copal wood and painted bright green with topaz eyes. A Chinantec woman poised in a crimson blouse embroidered with rainbow geometries that held the history of her family. I filled my pockets with these gems and sank my toes into a rich, loamy earth. I breathed in the scent of freshly opened ferns and squash blossom soup with herbs from the mountainside, set to a soundtrack of percolating marimbas and the buzz of cicadas before rain. Oaxaca brought my heart close to the surface.

I expected to stay for six months to detox from the corporate world, then move on. I stayed for three years. Oaxaca gave me no reason to leave. As so often happens when we put ourselves where we are supposed to be, doors begin to open. Shortly after arriving, I was offered a place to stay in the village as a live-in caretaker and property manager for an elderly man, an expatriate English professor from New York. Russell Ames left the United States with his wife, Jean, during the McCarthy era, finding Oaxaca more accepting of their radical choices. Nearly a year before my arrival, Russell had become a widower after more than forty years with his beloved Jean. Though five years his senior, Jean at 92 had been the stronger one. Alone, Russell needed assistance with the administration of his home, to drive him to the doctor in an old Renault the color of Pepto-Bismol, and to listen to stories of Big Bill Broonzy and songs of the Temperance Era. I resisted initially, not wanting to detour from my plan to become more immersed in local life, but I soon realized that Russell and Jean had been a part of San Pablo's history for generations and Casa Ames provided an integrated base from which to link to the community.

I lifted a heavy photo album from under the coffee table in Russell's living room and opened the frayed linen cover. The black and white photographs were mounted in corner tabs, gold and black, on pages dulled with age, ruffled and torn at the edges. Occasional titles appeared in fountain pen, in a feminine hand. *"Casa Ames 1959—Here We Go!"* The land was barren then. The first photo shows a sunset looking out over the valley to the languid mountains in the distance. No swimming pool yet, no pines, no shrubs in the shape of peacocks. Dark-skinned workers with hand tools smile in the scrubby foreground, rocks at their feet. Opposite is a photo of Jean in a polka dot dress with large white buttons, wearing a wide-brimmed straw hat—not a sombrero—the style of hat that women wore in the 50s. She balances on an unfinished adobe wall that was to form part of the fountained interior patio. Her arms reach out as if she intends to fly, and her face is in shadow but she appears to wink at the camera. In another photo Russell wears a white t-shirt, and holds two kittens that might be orange tabbies, and might be trying to squirm away. He looks beseechingly at the camera. *"Tell me what to do."* The captions say that in these first photos of their life in San Pablo, Jean was 52 and Russell 47. They were newlyweds, new expatriates and new landowners. As I turned the pages into more color-imagined memories of their lives together, the afternoon light in the living room settled on a carved wooden armadillo painted in dream-tones of aqua and tangerine, at the base of the wide stone fireplace. I closed the album and entered Russell's room.

"Okay, I'll stay." My curiosity was in a stranglehold. I wanted to know more of their colorful alternative story.

Later I learned from Russell that Jean's dress was a liquid shade of green, size six, and that her straw hat had a veil tucked up inside. That the rambunctious kittens were named "Tristan" and "Isolde" and one was eaten by an English Mastiff named "Sweetie." That the workers were local villagers, and though they had never before raised a house so grand, their skills measured worthy of the Taj Majal. Russell and Jean would eventually stand before the Taj Majal and deem it inferior to their own monument to love for lacking a sense of humor. He said they kept shovels in the trunk of the car, ready to uproot pines and vines and flowering trees from the side of the road for a new home in Casa Ames, preferring transplants for their tenacity. He said Jean adored that view of the mountains in the distance, and he served her perfectly cooked morning eggs—shirred or soft boiled in china egg cups—on the round table in the dining room, so she could start her days dreaming out the wide windows. For forty years.

Keeping Russell healthy and content in the home that was a main character in the story of his life, formed the thrust of my responsibility in Casa Ames. Nearing ninety when we met, in the year he spent as a new widower he moved into the world created by the memories of Jean and the life they shared in their home. He took solace in walking along the same paths that had guided his steps for those forty years. Every day he and his old dog, Nico, shuffled slowly on their spindly-stiff legs toward the road, where they would pause at the entrance to greet children and cows ambling by. Russell in his straw hat, deliberate, long and lean, tall as a ceiba. He carried two wooden walking sticks, and poked at twigs fallen from the pines to clear his way.

"Listen to the birds, Nico—'I love French perfume!' they sing."

Nico was a doggish version of Russell, long, lean and deliberate as a dog can be. To see them walking together inspired rhapsodies on companionship. Russell's senses remained sharp, though Nico was nearly blind at ninety-eight in dog years. If their step lacked steadiness, their friendship didn't.

At a bend the dirt road that led to an abandoned seminary, where neighbors stopped to rest, a sign was nailed to a tree. "Casa Ames." It sounded like "ah-mess" when pronounced in Spanish. The property's entrance had a hand-hewn wooden gate that never closed. Inside the property, just off the road, sat a compact caretaker's home that Russell had left for old, crusty Joe and his wife Dorothy. Joe used to care for Casa Ames and its visitors when Russell and Jean traveled to Turkey and Rome on home exchanges with money earned from the sale of parcels of their land. Joe was an electrician by trade, a grouch by hobby. He unfailingly upheld a vow of silence with Russell—some old squabble about the pink Renault. The tiny house had one bedroom, a bathroom, living room and a kitchen barely enough for two, or one and a half as Joe used to say, diminishing Dorothy in a manner he had perfected over decades. She never seemed to have unfurled entirely, tacked on to Joe's side, hands clenched in the pockets of her pilled sweaters. They sat in stackable plastic chairs at the entrance, smoking cigarettes and drinking beers. When anyone other than Russell passed by, they raised a bony hand to wave, but rarely said a word, ancient and mute as mummies.

A graceful stone step-way traced a contour of the land from behind Joe and Dorothy's house down to the "Casa Chica." Once a stable for Bernice, a mottled brown and white dairy cow, the house consisted now of just one room and a bath, with a patio of matching size that overlooked a valley where metal bells clanged and young herders mimicked goat sounds to nudge them along. *"Maaa!"* Sometimes the boys sounded like goats, sometimes the goats sounded like boys. John and his writerly girlfriend, Beth, lived in the tiny house. John was the quintessential hippie poet rug dealer cool guitar-playing Kerouac-type blues artist painter with a heart the size of Jupiter and a Buddhist-type acceptance of life's little pitfalls. About which he knew a bit. Beth credited Maximon, the cigar-smoking, whisky-drinking cravat-wearing Guatemalan devil deity for bringing them together. She had asked him for a favor. Just one good man, after… well, after all that stuff that made her writing so good. John qualified as her miracle, and he loved her in return as his own. After Jean's death, John spent a lot of time with Russell, editing letters to his alma mater, Columbia University, in which he suggested creative curriculum changes for the new millennium. Or reading Neruda's poetry to him in English and in Spanish. Russell was generous with the space on his land when friends needed it. The "Casa Chica" was *chica*, but that patio fully compensated for the house's diminutive size, with a view to the soft, low mountains in the west, and the strong, pregnant bulk to the east that birthed suns and moons in silence.

The main house sat under a scallop of red tiles and a ruffle of shade from jacarandas and creeping jasmines held high on wooden trellises. The lime-washed adobe house was low and lush. One, two, three short steps into the sunken patio garden at the entrance: an intentional ploy designed by Jean to induce contemplation. Don't rush into this home, please. You can touch the velvet blush of roses as you catch your breath. Russell did. The garden scattered a veil of confetti—well-tended, stocked, trimmed, fertilized and watered by Javier, Russell's gardener, who sometimes dug a little too deep. Any question from a gardener about the employer's bank account is ill-advised, and Javier asked many. Russell wore his post too proudly to say that the source of Javier's paychecks had long ago shriveled to just-enough, boosted twice a year by his children. But Javier kept a good garden, thriving with sun-loving lilies and cool shade begonias, all tucked into the right places, in slightly raised, irregular stone islands. Pots on the wide sills trailed succulents and lady slipper orchids—the windows thrown open so as not to miss the breeze that carried a scent of passionflower. The cats slept there, meditative donuts breathing in, breathing out.

Jean brought a piano across the ocean from her native France when she was ten, then 42 years later, up the dirt road to Casa Ames. With that piano, 100 years old when I sat on its bench, she introduced Shostakovich and Schubert to the Oaxacan countryside. Visitors dined on *Poulet a la Crème* from her gourmet kitchen, at a table set with dinnerware of delicate blue-tinted glass. By the time I accepted the accommodations with Russell, the house had fallen silent and the kitchen served cereal and sandwiches, though still on fine dinnerware. Russell spent his days re-reading travel journals of their trips to Czechoslovakia, Argentina and China. Strewn about the empty expanse of his king-sized bed, were Pablo Neruda's autobiography, several books by Richard Feynman, his own book on American Folk Music, and his Ph.D thesis "Citizen Thomas More and his Utopia" from Columbia University, 1949. Jean's bark paper collage of quetzal birds hung on the wall behind Russell, long tail feathers rising like plumes of memory from his gray head as he reclined, reading.

He no longer walked through much of the land where they had called forth their own utopia. The grounds reverted back to scrub. The terraced garden around the side of the house lay fallow. Dusty and curiously sparse pines surrounded the empty swimming pool with the green tile sea demons designed by Jean. The peacock shrubs were gangly, wayward branches. The duck pond filled with pods, seeds and fallen leaves from the ceibas that dotted the property. Jean's ashes lay under a patch of blue spring—a single forget-me-not that bloomed out back in the garden that Russell rarely saw. But where he did walk, and only there, the roses were pruned and Javier added fertilizer to the poinsettias each year. Cows and burros grazed on the vast back lawn. The most picturesque days of Casa Ames had passed. They lived now in Russell's stories that filled the void left behind when the center of his world dissolved.

I brought my cats (raising the house population to four), and Nico didn't mind the dogs that followed me home after my morning walks or Nini, the puppy we adopted to succeed her. I had a place to write, a kitchen and garden to discover. And the freedom and time to do work I wanted to do. I found work everywhere. The agency for abused women needed a translator. The children's shelter needed a library aide. I worked online to disseminate news for indigenous dignity, translated for the indigenous cause, drove the pink Renault to help establish an events center in a centuries-old hacienda in a nearby town, and took the *gringo* neighbors to immigration and the Mexican neighbors to doctors. I oversaw construction and picked lettuce on an organic farm, sweet colorful bouquets of Lollo Rosso and Tom Thumb. I house sat. Fed cats. Visited Telmex to prod for phone lines for the community. I picked up garbage along the road. Installed Internet in a dozen households once the phone lines at long last arrived. I put ribbons around the neck of stray dogs and sat with them at the grocery store until a new family adopted them. Others came along in the front seat of the Renault, to the vet to be spayed. Finally freedom, finally time.

Shortly after I moved in with Russell, the friend I had walked with from Uruapan to Nuevo San Juan Parangaricútiro, also a tourism refugee, joined us at the dinner table, and accepted Russell's invitation to stay. Together, Janet and I resumed the tradition of producing interesting meals in Russell's kitchen, working from recipes from Jean's own hand-typed cookbook. I planted the terraced garden with carrots, Easter Egg radishes, lettuces, Thai Basil, turnips and Mini Pearl tomatoes, throwing in a handful of giant double zinnias in shades of pink and copper. Janet polished and scrubbed the house with the help of the staff. The heavy chef-quality pots that hung on an iron ring above the stove were accessible, but coated with a layer of grease. Why would Jean have chosen that spot? Because she cooked every day. Because when pots are used, enjoyed and regularly washed, no dulling film accumulates. Casa Ames lost a bit of the dark that had collected since Jean's death. Instead of sandwiches and cereal, Russell had waffles and chicken curry with apples, raisins and cashews. Every Friday we invited John and Beth, and during the week, friends often brought magnificent home-cooked dinners and to-die-for dessert. Casa Ames transformed, again, into an enthralling place to gather. Russell reassumed his position at the center.

"Russell, you would have blushed to hear the song the girls sang at the library meeting!"

"Hard to make me blush these days—what did they sing?"

"A saucy song about lewd and lascivious men…"

"Oh, *that* one! I *taught* them that!"

There are times in life when abundant love falls within easy reach. Casa Ames basked in love. Not because of Russell, or because of us, because of the past or because of the generous neighbors, both Mexican and *gringo*, or the gentle community around us. Love bloomed bountiful in Casa Ames because we had time to experience it. We weren't rushing off to another place. We were all right there.

This corner of Oaxaca had been Russell and Jean's willing canvas for decades, and when nearing their 80s they imagined the land with a future as bright as its past. Academics both, they had a good relationship with the bilingual university based in Mexico City, and in 1984 Jean began the proceedings to bequeath the land to the university, retaining rights to stay on the premises until their deaths. Friends and family applauded their decision. Russell's children had visited over the years, but didn't express any interest in bonding with the land that had kept their father so distant. Neighbors were content to know that the lush space that had become a part of the San Pablo landscape would not fall into the hands of wrong-headed people.

The entire village knew the story of the land. The man who led his tawny oxen to graze in the grassy mountainside knew it. The official who collected the $10 a year for water fees knew it. Russell's long-standing staff of three who cooked, cleaned, and gardened knew it, and so did the mayor. People repeated the story as legend. As it was known to the community that Russell and Jean had long ago brought them electricity and water, helped build a school, and distributed candy every year on Children's Day, so it was known that Jean and Russell would die in their home and a school would grow as their legacy. In the year 2000, at 92 years old, Jean died and left Russell alone to tend the memories at Casa Ames and continue their link with the community.

Living in Casa Ames, Janet and I formed a part of that link. Russell, the house and land were a reference point in the village's tradition and language.

"It's up past Casa Ames."

"Back when Casa Ames dug the second well…"

"You know, when my father worked for Señor Ames…"

"Don Russell will remember when the stream ran behind the house…"

While Russell's world condensed as he dwelled more and more in memory, the arms of the community hugged tighter around him. His former housekeeper, retired for a decade, visited with a basket of soft mangoes. He gave her a carved wooden bird when she left. The man who had done the paperwork for Jean's license renewals shared an afternoon beer. He left with a book on Finnish metalwork. Friends visited to play the piano or bring Russell news from the city. People cared for him, gently and truly, because the roots he and Jean had set down reached far beneath the dirt streets and collective history of this place.

To the expats in the greater Oaxaca community, the Ames were the venerated old guard. Those in San Pablo were close and supportive, part of an extended family. I didn't know much about the greater expat community in Oaxaca, except as linked through Russell. I met many good people who had adopted Mexico as their home but close as I became to this retired and settled community through my association with Casa Ames, I still had a great deal of my Mexico to discover.

SCATTERING WORDS ON THE WIND

From Oaxaca to Chiapas

In the summer of 2001 I traveled to Chiapas for a month while Janet kept Casa Ames running. Chiapas borders Oaxaca, and is the birthplace of the pan-indigenous movement opened by the Zapatistas in 1994. Mexico cherishes the indigenous, when their scarlet-hued folklore and original handicrafts serve as a magnet for tourists. In reality, many marginalized indigenous live on lands that hold some of the richest resources in timber, minerals and water, which gives them official "obstacle" status. The indigenous movement seeks to reclaim an undisputed space for Mexico's original people, one not still stained in tones of conquest. I respected the insistence and creativity of the movement: indigenous people used traditional methods of education and communal consent to create systems and supports for their remote communities, where the government was unwilling to provide or destroyed through neglect. Many communities were tricked or violently forced off their ancestral lands rich in resources, much like the history of the indigenous in the U.S. The response from the indigenous communities, once subsided the initial uprising and "declaration of war" in 1994, has not been violent. Communities set up new homes, new schools and started again.

In Chiapas I slept on the ground in a Mayan encampment of displaced families at Nuevo Yibeljoj. On that first night inside indigenous territories, a veil of mosquitoes drifted across my eyes and cheeks, and I felt the earth lumped under my sleeping bag. Under the *tulipan* tree that served as the community center, an old man sat on a rock, the rhythm of his guitar escorted the slow passage of a gibbous moon. The thin light thrown by a votive placed in prayer before the *Virgen de Guadalupe* on an altar outside my sleeping quarters danced with the beams on the ceiling. In this remote encampment of families who escaped violence in their villages, the stirring of the guitar strings, the mosquitoes and the candlelight kept me from sleep. Now I was the visitor in a world far more foreign than any I had known, and I wanted to see beyond what I read in the books and saw from my safe quarters.

I walked to the latrine a hundred paces away in the mud created by the chill Sierra Madre rains, through a glittering curtain of fireflies. The moon hid behind clouds that hung low around mountains whose reassuring mineral presence was magnetizing, even in the dark. Far from the noise of modern technology, you can hear a mountain hum. In this indigenous Mexico that bore no resemblance to anything I had experienced before, however remote, I had to pay close attention to keep my balance. Nothing was recognizable, and much was not as it appeared. The fireflies became pinpoint stars, and as I waved my hand through the sky in front of my eyes, the constellations rearranged.

From Nuevo Yibeljoj I travelled to La Realidad, a Zapatista town run by the autonomous authority. With a letter of consent from a solidary agency, I knocked on a secret door in San Cristobal de las Casas, where they processed me, paired me with companions for travel, and oriented us on our role as observers. We were to document the incursion of the military in indigenous zones. We were given a "passport" that would allow us entry into the Zapatista community, but were to hide it in our shoe, or some other place safe from possible discovery along the way at checkpoints. It wasn't illegal to travel into Zapatista territory, but authorities might attempt to dissuade us, aware that observers were there essentially to watch the government, and usually had links to press. From the back of a cargo truck for over eight hours on an improvised road of mud that seemed at times like quicksand, I witnessed some of the most beautiful and remote countryside I have seen in Mexico, ducking to avoid tree limbs that overhung the road, and craning to catch a glimpse of waterfall racing down the side of a velvet green mountain. We stopped frequently to push ourselves free of the muck, amid frothy, foaming mounds of jungle and bird calls that hinted at resplendent feathers.

By day I bathed in a cold whirlpool ringed by ferns, swept, carried firewood for cooking and worked in the heat of the sun. I wrote under trees whose branches embraced raucous toucans and cascading wild orchids. Children drew turkeys and monkeys and masked men in my notebook. The young learned Spanish, but I didn't speak the Tzeltal language of their parents. We communicated as anyone does who has encountered a friendly foreigner—signs and smiles and the few words of Spanish they knew. "Banana." "Coffee." "River." "Snake."

I chose to visit these communities because of the volunteer work I had done involving the indigenous struggle, and because it presented a new challenge to find my way in an unfamiliar context. At the end of a month, I had not found my way. I found *other* ways, which involved solidarity and the willingness to pull a bud of hope, magician-like, out of thin air—ways which I filed away for future reference, not knowing then that one day I would become dependent on that belief in the extraordinary power of people working together, of hope springing from the most unlikely of places.

These communities decided to uproot themselves from the ooze of government oppression and paramilitary violence in their home-villages, march far with few belongings, and carve a new life in the jungle in search of the luxury of safety and self-determination. It was brave and dignified work, this beginning again. Even with blood so fresh in their past, they sang melodious stories as they worked so the children would not forget.

Jose Santis and his family had heard the screams of massacre. Sounds that I could not imagine exploded in his ears. The scent of blood ran through his village in waves, briny as the sea. He held his tiny daughter's delicate hand and drew her close, whispering words that made the girl smile, then laugh, then whisper back.

"We were once kings," he said.

"And I was once a child," she returned.

Working the earth with their hands and feet and spirits, they tended to their corn in torrents of rain and sang hope into their days. From what I could discern through my tiny keyhole, the specific gravity of this hope outweighed their despair.

The tiny discomforts I chose to endure, sleeping on the ground and bearing calluses on my palms as I worked, were meager attempts to feel the earthen life through the small of my back—not only through my eyes. I was though, only an observer. I would return to my cats, to serve them tender bits from a can. I would be home to Russell, where the roof over my head wasn't mine, but it was sturdy and I was welcome. Struck by their song and resolve in the face of a storm of great loss, I fought against focusing on the rainbow. Marginality may breed a certain tenacity that is as startling as it is magnificent, but I would not stay long enough in Chiapas to subsist on a ration of last year's wormy beans and coffee after a poor harvest. I would not bury a child because the herb poultices failed, and the doctor lived a twelve-hour walk away. I would not need to continually fight against the disappearance of a tenuous hope into the deep shadows, or worry that the water supply hold out through the dry season. Once home in my own dark what would I see?

In Chiapas I witnessed as a community faced their dark and pulled hope from it, lacing their daily lives with a luminous trust in themselves and in the future, in spite of having so few choices... or precisely because of it. I learned that the elusive heartbeat of the indigenous world extends far beyond what outsiders can appreciate from the swirl of their art's form and color in the local markets. *In situ*, this doggedness of spirit might only be possible in a people intimate with nature's ability to renew. In people who celebrate rain and rejoice when a sunflower's weary seeded head falls to the earth. In people who feel the very movement of the earth.

I slipped a smooth, freckled stone from La Realidad into my pocket, a reminder of durability and beauty produced by centuries of erosion.

A group of women sang—they traveled around Mexico and produced a CD. A savvy use of technology marks the new indigenous movement. They called themselves "Las Abejas"—the Bees. They learned songs in Spanish to present their stories to the public. If you didn't know, the songs sounded tender and cheerful. But translated from Tzeltal, they told of guns and power and the loss of lives so dear that only song could manage the retelling without tears.

"*Kohlabal.* Thank you" I said.

"Tell people about us." I believe this is what they said. I am not certain, but they pointed at me and made a sign like scattering words on the wind.

STORIES IN THE CORNERS

From Chiapas to Oaxaca

I wrote and published a few pieces about what I found in Chiapas in the month after my trip and before September 11, 2001. Then suddenly, the winds carried a more abrasive noise, overwhelming the music of the bees. On that day homologous with emergency, I told Russell at 11 am what I knew via a phone call from Janet who was visiting her home in Chicago—that planes had crashed into the World Trade Center and the Pentagon. He responded calmly, shaking his head.

"Well, it looks like another new era in history is beginning."

In nine decades, he had seen a few.

Russell was an observer and noted carefully the world around him. He once had me write to the publishers of National Geographic to ask them to put a wider white margin around the page, as the photos prevented him from writing notes about what he read. "Bromeliads in Paradise?" "Gnaturally Gnatty." "This rhino is a wino."

He kept a notebook by his bedside where he noted daily observations on his life and questions that he hoped to answer someday. His handwriting encoded his musings, but I could understand some… "…felt dizzy." "… like strawberries grow on shit." "Jean always said…" He tallied birds he saw from his window and returned my borrowed books annotated in the margins. "Aha!" with underlines and x's. This received two check marks in a book by David James Duncan:

"My topic is the grief and frenzy that daily invade every sincere human's attempts to simply pursue a vocation that expresses gratitude and respect for life."

Russell appeared to be grateful to a life that had afforded him luxuries. He was grateful to have forgotten the hurts, recalling doubts about his duties as a good father only when the wind was full and the words would quickly vanish. Grateful for Jean—for the forty years her music filled Casa Ames, and for her echo that spilled around corners, a tickle in his ears. He wrote a poem for her, a decade before her death at 92. In "Lady on the Shady Side of Eighty" Jean is in hell playing mean piano with the demons and demonesses, as Russell fans her with a page from "Romeo and Juliet." Abundant love, life and memory resided in Casa Ames. I could have stayed until the great ceibas fell away to dust, or until Russell decided that it was time for him to depart.

Early in 2003, we received papers that indicated that someone else thought it was already time for Russell to leave. If not this life, then at least the house, though after his decades there, the two were clearly synonymous to him. Russell was served papers from the Rector of the university to whom he and his wife had deeded their land. He was to pay back rent for the three years since Jean died, and was to leave the property within a period of time to be specified. It made no sense. Stunned, we turned to Tony for help. Tony was like family to Russell, and lived down the road in a Bed and Breakfast that his parents built just after Russell and Jean settled in the town—the location the poets used for their writing retreats. Tony was in touch with Russell's children and knew Russell's history, having grown up with Russell and Jean as mentors. Though my responsibility was to Russell and the house, it stopped short of interpreting legal situations, as I had carefully steered clear of anything that might indicate I had interest other than to care for Russell and the house as a caregiver and friend. Friends in town had repeatedly suggested that I obtain a

Power of Attorney to be able to claim mail that arrived registered or otherwise assist Russell when his limited mobility was an impediment. I chose not to involve myself in his legal matters, and now with the claim of the university in hand, hoped that Tony would be able to communicate with Russell's children or handle the situation himself. He sought a lawyer, and kept us informed of the civil proceedings as needed. With a laymen's knowledge of the Mexican judicial system, we knew that cases could languish for a good while, and only hoped that the whole thing would take long enough that Russell would be allowed to peacefully pass away amidst the stories lingering in the corners of Casa Ames.

When Tony came up with the idea to sue the university and reclaim the land, he discussed this with the lawyer and tried to bring Russell on board.

"Why would you want to do that, Tony?"

"So the land doesn't fall into the hands of evil people!"

"But who would care for it? My kids aren't interested. Who?"

Tony said not to worry, that the land could be sold to someone more caring. But I had a bad feeling from the start. My gut told me to just fight the real battle. Russell needs to stay on his land until he dies. That is the battle. It was forever understood that the university would have the land after Russell's death. Trying to turn that around seemed to blur the picture and take the focus off of Russell's right to remain. But I had relinquished any real involvement in the legalities of the civil suit. I had turned it over to Tony. It was indeed languishing though. Months passed and we were informed that the case was still stuck in some or another stage that didn't mean yet that Russell owed any money or had to leave. It was enough for the time being.

I woke every morning before dawn to walk in the mountains. I needed my mornings, like love, like water. I tiptoed from my bedroom to Russell's room where the dog slept. Nini was no longer a puppy, and spilled over with joy in the morning, always ready at the door to leap onto my chest. Often, several other neighborhood dogs would join us along the way. Rat, Lobo, Otto, Lukas. Depending on the season, I either heard my footsteps or not. Depending on the moon, I either saw the path or not. Depending on the number of dogs, I either had one beside me or not, as they were prone to canine group elation and scavenger hunts.

The insects buzzed in the bushes and trees, soothing night sounds. I felt proprietary about the path at that hour. It was a different space in the morning than it was as the day wore on, when men from town headed up with burros to collect wood, or led their cattle up to graze. In the morning it was my path, a space I entered with my dogs that no one else knew about. Though the path was sparsely illuminated, I walked with a length of bamboo to steady my step, reminding myself that I could fall no further than the ground beneath my feet.

Passing the old seminary, the graded road ended, and we climbed on a small footpath, at times gravel, at times rock, at times spongy weed moistened by the stream that grew and receded with the seasons. Ferns lined a part of the path that entered forest, large green ferns and small ferns like fists, that stayed closed in the dry season, and opened to velvet in the rainy season. Spider webs tangled in my eyelashes—I pleaded forgiveness for recklessly destroying their dreams. The sky changed from onyx to pearl, and the hum of the morning turned melodic as insects stowed themselves away and birds awakened. There is a particular kind of birdsong that occurs pre-dawn, perhaps because there is little other sound to compete and the air is clear. Perhaps the birds feel freedom to sing all the notes in their repertoire at once. That particular coincidence of jeweled sky with a full-on avian opera is more special to me than a night at the Met. And I had it every day.

Our destination was a large white rock in the side of the mountain, on the hips of a vertical meadow. There, the dogs came round again, as I sat for twenty minutes to just breathe, eyes closed, Nini's head on my lap, protected in a semi-circle of panting tongues that would make sure no harm befell me unaware.

There was absolutely nothing missing.

IN DIZZY SPIRALS

From Oaxaca to New York and back

Then there was Bill.

In mid-September in New York, the days are not certain which side of the season to cling to—do they hang on to summer's laze or tip toward the zeal of autumn? The giant mounds of sweet corn in the August markets are reduced to meager heaps; the split hides of the few remaining tomatoes belie their sweetness. Bill ran by the farmer's market in Union Square for four ears of corn and an ugly tomato before he met me at the bus from Kennedy Airport.

I had traveled to New York City to see.

Bill was the writer with whom I shared tea at the writing retreat in Oaxaca in 1999. The one who told me there can be future in writing. He wrote edgy city stories. I wrote dreamy Mexican tales. We were both coming out of relationships and going into new jobs when we met, but had enough in common to keep us talking over chamomile tea late at night, of those topics that new friends explore—childhood, favorite books, travel, family—listening to the dogs bark off in the distance during the pauses when we considered more intimate subjects. Then we talked about the barking dogs.

We kept in vague contact. Author stuff. He was doing a reading, I published a poem. Bill returned to Oaxaca for a writing retreat in the summer of 2003. I had lived in San Pablo for three years by then, and Casa Ames was down the dirt road from the writers' space. I contracted with my poet-friend Donna, to arrange transportation, tours and meals for the writers in exchange for writing with the group. I could handle that relaxed tourism, as it gave me time to walk with the dogs and fix dinner for Russell. In ten days Bill and I had time to remember our friendship. We laughed over jokes that few others understood, and talked about burros in Manhattan and skyscrapers in San Pablo. He wrote a poem whose rhythm stayed in my head, and later said he wrote it for me.

On the day before his departure, we drove to an artisan village in Russell's pink Renault, where Bill bought a coyote carved from copal wood, painted purple with bright yellow sunbursts on his back. I think he had blue eyes. Bill's were somewhere between fertile earth and restless sea.

I am not certain when it started to feel different. We paid a dollar to enter a plaza lined with mezcal booths and drank all we could handle, making faces at each other when we downed the shot glasses in one gulp. On a sun laced patio, over *pescado a la veracruzana* we fashioned bugs from napkins—he a spider, me a worm. It could have been on the drive home, when we turned to each other to acknowledge the delight of the day, and his smile spotlighted a hole in my idyllic life. I slept and woke in dizzy spirals that night, dreaming asleep and dreaming awake. The next morning Bill visited for pre-dawn tea. We put a few words and a few kisses to the feelings that had tangled into the previous ten days. I drove him to the airport, and he flew from gritty Oaxaca, over the turbulent Gulf of Mexico, miles up the Eastern Seaboard and home to his wilds of Manhattan.

A few weeks later, I went to see. He invited me to write with him at a retreat on the coast of Massachusetts. We wrote by the mudflats, then held hands on Broadway, in delis, at Ground Zero and Sheep Meadow, and sailed on the Long Island Sound in his boat named Panda as the late afternoon sun smeared the sky with faded peony tones. We talked past a few of the barking dogs, and I buckled at the discovery that Mexico had not given me all I needed. In Bill I perceived a confident man with a life full and vibrant—he didn't need me. And I did not need him. But I knew that I wanted to figure out life's big puzzles with a partner. I wanted to be on a team. Again drawn to the mysterious, for the first time in seventeen years I considered part of my life outside Mexico, for a part of my life in Mexico suddenly seemed deficient. Before I left, I hid notes in his apartment. *"Thanks for you and New York."* I wrote in small, sure script in tiny books handmade by Jean that Russell had given me before I left "just in case."

There is a photograph that Bill's timed camera took of us on Panda. We smile, curled around each other, content. Weeks later it appeared in my hometown Schenectady Gazette under the front-page headline "Local Woman Moves to Mexico to Find a Story—and Becomes One."

Less than a week after I returned to San Pablo from our explorations in New York, my head and heart pleasantly discombobulated, the earth shifted, again, and I fell into the chasm of a change that—this time—I did not choose.

EVERYTHING POSSIBLE

From Oaxaca to Ixcotel

On that Monday night, I did not ensure that Russell, one week into his ninety-second year, was safely tucked into his book-strewn bed at nine-thirty, as I had every night for three years. I did not bring a biscuit to Nini at the foot of his bed, scratching her tummy and promising her the walk in the mountains early the next morning, as I had done every night for three years. I did not turn off the computer in my writing studio, full of Russell's dusty volumes. I did not write Bill the nightly email. Before going to bed, I did not set the breakfast table for Russell, with his pink and white pills on a demitasse saucer, alongside the petaled plate where his blue-eyed Siamese cat would share his bacon. And I didn't ease into the comfort of my own bed to read Carlos Fuentes before sleep, pausing before my view of the mountain washed in moonlight, framed by the jacaranda tree outside my window. I did not pull the thick woven blanket around me. I did not breathe in the age of its heavy wool, as I had every night for three years.

That night I lay on a concrete floor that smelled of insecticide in the Oaxaca State Penitentiary in the town of Ixcotel, on a garish blue Tweety Bird blanket taunting "Pleasant Dreams" in fancy cursive. It was almost midnight by the time I was led down an exterior corridor, following two guards dressed in black and whole families of scuttling rats. They led me to an unused office, with a rusty sink clogged with gray paint chipped off a crumbling wall. A half-empty snack-sized bag of chili-lemon corn chips was thrown in one corner and in the other, that Tweety blanket barely fit in the narrowness of the room. Hoarse groans and the sound of a flushing toilet filtered through a barred window near the ceiling.

The photos and fingerprints were done, the body searches and the medical history. Tired clerks had filled out forms in triplicate, pecking officiously on tinny manual typewriters. No, I have no tattoos. Yes, I attended college. No, I have no specified religion. Yes, I am in Mexico legally. Finally alone, I splashed cold water on my face and fell against the wall, sliding to the floor, dripping. *Tranquila.* It will be fine in the morning. Friends will send a lawyer, apologies around, and I will return home. I worried about Russell. I wanted to sleep so the night would pass quickly; so this would be over. I lay down with Tweety and steadied my breath, bobbing fitfully between dream and reality. The crickets I dreamed under my jacaranda turned shrill and sharp as the guards whistled signals throughout the night. The lone owl on the branch of the ceiba tree by Russell's tool shed screeched and took off on a great flutter of wings for the dark woods, but it just was the guards keeping vigil in the outer corridor, goofing off, playing tag and singing falsetto to love songs along with their radio. I had no pillow to blunt the reality that invaded my dreams.

That Monday night, Russell was finishing his black bean soup with a square of buttered cornbread. He told me again about Wabash College and the A the second-year French professor had promised him but reneged on. Janet was away on vacation.

Though I knew the story by heart, I prodded him to continue.

"What happened, Russell? Why didn't she come through with the A?"

At 7 pm he was almost ready for his vanilla ice cream with homemade chocolate sauce. Lobo barked outside. Lobo was a neighbor's dog, an imposing husky-like guy with a gentle heart, one blue eye and one honey-colored. He loved Russell for the dog treats he kept in the pocket of his guayabera-shirt, and me for the bones I sneaked out the back door to him when the other dogs weren't around. He often jumped through my open bedroom window at night and settled his big bear of a black dog body where I wouldn't miss him on my way out to walk the next morning. During the day, he dozed in the shade of a luxuriant jasmine bush at the entrance and guarded the house as if it were his own, which, to a dog's manner of thinking, it might have been. He had taken possession, but nobody minded.

"Hang on to that answer for a minute, Russell. Lobo's making a fuss. There must be somebody here. I'll be right back."

About thirty feet from the front door, Lobo leapt in circles around two men swinging at him nervously with branches broken off our ceiba tree.

"*Shhhh, bájate, Lobo… ¿En qué les puedo ayudar?*"

"So you speak Spanish. Call off your dog."

"He's not my dog, and he doesn't like men with sticks. How can I help you?"

I had not seen these men before. I bristled because they yanked pieces off our tree and greeted me with a command in my own home. I hoped I wouldn't have to summon Lobo's bulk, but I knew I could trust it.

"We need you to answer a few questions with Joe."

"Joe?"

Joe was a hermit, and I had little contact with him outside of the occasional wave and having once been called by him to twist the wedding ring from Dorothy's cold finger after she died. "And get her watch too." Even as she finally claimed her independence from Joe, he brushed her aside. When I brought her cremated remains from the funeral home, packaged in a box labeled "Moisturizing Hand

Cream," Joe flicked the ash from his cigarette on the floor, punted the box under the couch and muttered "Dust to dust." He was a man of few words, and most of them acid.

"Call off your dog, we said!"

"*Lobo, tranquilo.*" He sat at my feet but didn't remove his eyes from the sticks. "I'm sorry. I don't know much about Joe. Are you sure you have the right person?"

And they said my name. First and last. It sounded like "Moddy Helen Sanher"—but it was clearly my name, written on a scrap of paper. I didn't think Joe knew my last name—nobody did. I didn't need a last name in this tiny town of farms and goatherds. I'm not sure even Russell could remember my last name, and I had been his caregiver, staff administrator, and friend for three years.

They removed badges from their pockets and said they were federal "preventive" police. They wore no uniforms, and I couldn't figure out what they wanted to prevent. What could I possibly have to do with Joe?

"Is Joe okay?"

"We'll ask the questions. Now let's go."

Their disruption annoyed me and I was anxious to resume my routine. My responsibility to Russell clearly trumped their agenda, no matter how insistent.

"You'll have to wait because I left Mr. Ames inside expecting his dessert, and he can't be left alone. So if you'll excuse me, you can return in a half hour and I'll try to help you."

They moved closer.

"Look, we won't wait a half hour or a half minute. We've asked you nicely. Let's go, and there won't be any violence."

Violence. They might as well have told me they were bringing in circus elephants. Minutes ago, my most perplexing question was why that A in French mattered so much to Russell after seventy-five years. Violence? I didn't dare take my gaze off theirs. I echoed the absurdity of their suggestion.

"No, of course there won't be any violence. I've already told you that I'll answer whatever I can. But I will take care of Mr. Ames first. Now you will excuse me..."

And I walked away from them. I needed to serve Russell his vanilla ice cream. It was the only action that made sense at that moment. I needed to be inside the house. I let them follow me to prove I was not lying.

"I'll be right with you, Russell!" I motioned my arm toward where he sat staring out the window at his dimming valley, my gesture meant to convey "See?"

They followed me to the freezer, to the heavy pan with the homemade chocolate sauce, and back to Russell's round table.

"Ho Ho! Who are these fine men?" He must not have noticed the sticks.

I presented the men to Russell as officials who were trying to help Joe with something. They put their sticks behind their back to shake Russell's hand.

"Russell, these men need my help with some questions."

"She's pretty smart. You came to the right place." Russell talked to the men, but he looked at me with a question in his eyes.

I asked how long we would be. They stood too close to Russell.

"Half an hour. That's all it will take. Yes, half an hour or so."

"I'll be back in half an hour, Russell. How 'bout you eat your ice cream in your bedroom?"

I had perceived these two men as one. They arrived together, both held broken branches, both knew my full name, both followed me. I remember no details of their individual appearance. They were the collective police with a collective purpose that I couldn't yet grasp. But when I headed to the bedroom with the cut crystal bowl of softening vanilla ice cream, one official, who was no different from the other, said to the other, who was no different from the first, "Follow her."

He trailed me wordlessly as I placed the ice cream by Russell's bed, and walked back to the dining room. They stood aside and watched as I helped Russell out of his chair and positioned his walker. Then we filed slowly, matching Russell's pace, along the cool red slab tiles that he and Jean had chosen for their garden-edged patio when they built their home. We walked into his bedroom by the wall of rose-colored river rocks that formed his fireplace.

"Jean and I spent days collecting the prettiest pink stones back where the stream used to run," Russell explained to the men. "And I personally supervised the masons for three days while they built this, so they placed each one with its best face forward. They were artists! See? *Muy bonito.*"

Russell's Spanish was dignified and well-practiced. He told that story a thousand times, sometimes concluding with *"Fabuloso."* In his comfortable role as host he showed them one of the miniature hand-fashioned books where Jean had left him love notes, and I tugged his drapes shut, reminding him I wouldn't be gone long.

Three years earlier, Russell had awakened on a Tuesday morning to find Jean still and silent beside him in the bed where they had slept, sang, and told stories by the rose-colored fireplace. After his many years in Mexico, Russell knew about the fault lines. How one moment can change your life forever. He recovered from her death, but he didn't recover from living without her. His world quieted and darkened, and he often spoke of the sunlight illuminating the tiny golden hairs on Jean's arms.

"Let's go, let's go," one of the men snarled.

"See you in a bit, Russell."

They stood too close on either side of me as we walked together along the dirt driveway for the hundred feet to Joe's house.

We never arrived.

To one side of Joe's house, three cars and at least five more men in street clothes blocked the entrance by the hand-painted wooden sign that said "Casa Ames," arms crossed in front of their puffed chests.

"Get in the car."

They asked no questions. The questions in the air were mine now.

They had three of us. Old acid Joe, John, and me.

"I'm not getting in that car. I can't leave Russell and I have no idea what you want."

The brawniest guy ordered the second brawniest to get the handcuffs.

"Do you guys have wives? Mothers? Sisters? Would you recommend that they get in a car with guys that they don't know—guys carrying sticks?"

I had once ridden a bus between Acapulco and Ixtapa where we were held up at gunpoint. Feeling the steel barrel push against my temple, I knew that I should give in—give them what they wanted.

The bus bandit stuck his hand down the front of my shirt, and I grabbed it and threw it aside, indignant.

He grabbed my purse. If I let them have my wallet they would have the picture of my mother and me taken before she was wheeled into heart surgery.

"You can have the money but I need the wallet back."

"Shut up or I'll put a bullet through your head."

That should have been enough.

"It has a picture of my mother—it means nothing to you."

He took about $80 and threw my wallet back, unknowingly leaving me my treasured photo and enough for taxi fare to get myself home from the bus terminal. The sixteen-year-old in the window seat next to me told me I was foolish and offered me a piece of gum. "They shoot, you know."

The cocky defensiveness from that bus returned, as the men sent for the handcuffs. This time no gun was pointed at my temple but I felt again that a force uninvited was threatening something dear to me. I replayed the same foolish stomp of my foot and defiant plant of my chin—*What right do you have to take this from me? It means nothing to you...*

I asked for documentation that would indicate why we were corralled for questioning. They showed me an arrest warrant. The charge on paper said, "Arrest for conspiracy to overtake land." I recognized the word—*despojo*—from my work translating documents about indigenous people who were tricked off their lands. Now it seemed we were the ones being tricked. The warrant was issued by the same university in Mexico City that had accepted Russell and Jean's donation of their property twenty years ago. The same university that claimed Russell should leave the land, and was currently being sued by Tony and the lawyer.

Unable to puzzle the pieces together as I knew so little about the case, I trusted it was a case of crossed wires, a misunderstanding. We obviously had Russell's permission to be with him on the land, and as he was not yet dead, the land was his. Take it over? We knew the story—ask anybody. Ask the mayor. Ask Maria who washes her clothes by hand in her yard across the road. Ask old man Hector on his walk to church. The entire town knew. The land belonged to him while he lived. That was our only conspiracy—keeping him alive and content in his home as long as he wanted. Lines had tangled. Perhaps this grew out of the civil suit, and some lawyer was confused. If we answered their questions, it would be clear.

When John's girlfriend, Beth, consented to sit with Russell while we straightened this out, we got in the car, avoiding handcuffs but shoved by men who were too big to need to shove.

I asked the officer who was driving if someone from the precinct would drive us home after the questioning. It still astounds me. I assumed that nothing transcendent could happen to us as innocent people. It more than astounds me that I had so little gut feeling—about armed police who threaten to beat my dog, handcuff me and drag me away from my home. But we were *innocent*, you see... My trust was in that innocence.

At police headquarters, we were locked behind bars in separate cells. There were, of course, no questions. We were allowed one phone call. Having no numbers on hand, I called Tony. As he was working with Russell's lawyer on the civil case and friends with the consular agent, I thought the three of them could make the necessary calls to put the monster back into its cage.

An hour later, in the back of an enclosed truck, after the first of many sets of photos and fingerprints, we were transported from police headquarters to Ixcotel. No questions asked. Joe and John smoked, and I carved my initials and the year into the layers of green paint that coated the walls, between "Jose loves Ana" and "I am your mother and I am here," a reference to the *Virgen de Guadalupe*, the great protectress of Mexicans for troubles and tribulations from athlete's foot to incarceration to crossing the border. "MES 2003." Joe commented on every pothole we slammed over. John and I laughed. A kind of rush takes hold when facing the implausible—like when the rock-solid ground under your feet quakes, or when you fall in love again. Scary, thrilling, implausible events can make you giddy, wondering what comes next and believing in your invincibility, at least while the rush lasts.

Joe wore a brown plaid shirt. John and I both wore red. I thought of the earthen pottery robins and sparrows on Russell's mantel. As writers, John and I noted our good fortune to be able to add a "night in jail" story to our repertoires. Joe groused that he already had plenty. We sat on wooden benches bolted into the sides of the truck, with no windows for us to see what direction we headed. It's not far, they had said, though time already waddled by at a different speed, and our perception of distance warped, finding no straight path to link wherever this would end to wherever it began. We didn't know where Ixcotel was, and I still don't. Somewhere past where the owl took off for the woods.

"You think those mug shots will show up in the paper? I want to send one home to my mom." John, the entertainer.

"Yeah, I can just see the kid who sells the *Noticias* on the corner of Chapultepec. They always open to the police section. "*Gringos* caught squatting!" If he's lucky he'll sell enough to buy himself two *tortas de jamón*." Joe, the cynic.

"I smiled. They pointed that damned camera at me, and I smiled." Me, caught in the sliver of disbelief between one reality and the next, neither one filtering into the close, smoke-filled air in the back of that rumbling truck.

I don't recall how many sliding, screeching, slamming doors we passed through that night, led by guards in black. In that sea of dark sounds, scents and movements I focused on what lie in front of me, for behind those bars swarmed rats, and on the other side of that wall I remembered home. I couldn't face the tally of what I was losing and gaining with every step. The physicals and questions were the business at hand. Answer. Breathe. Answer.

They asked for our wallets and John and Joe for their belts. I thought—so they wouldn't hang themselves. Isn't that how it goes in prisons? I had nothing with me, as I left the house thinking I was walking no farther than to Joe's.

"Do we need to take her watch? How bad are they inside?" the Director asked the guard of the women's compound.

"They are calm right now."

"Keep it."

Calm right now.

The doctor was a woman. She said my blood pressure read dangerously high. I told her I had not suffered from high blood pressure, but then I had not before been nabbed from my home on a pleasant evening to be shuffled off to prison without explanation and without dessert. She asked me what I did. I said "nothing." She asked me what I did for a living. I said I was a writer. She perked up—her daughter was a writer, too. On the corner of a message pad, she wrote her name and phone number, folded it smaller than a quarter, and told me to keep it secret, but to call should I "need her" for anything.

We were given private rooms with access to a shared bathroom. They assigned Joe a bed in the infirmary. He was 75 and had a hole in his jaw that dripped spittle. Throat cancer earned him extra-special dispensation. We received comforters so we wouldn't have to sleep against the cool stone of the floor, mine a bright yellow Tweety Bird against a pale blue sky with clouds, John's a dark green plaid. We assumed that these privileges indicated that our stay would be brief. I tried to ease the growing tension in my chest by closing my eyes and picturing the white rock where I sat in the mornings with my sentinel dogs, protecting me from harm. I tried the breathing exercises that there, on the mountainside, anchored me to the earth and to myself. I found no anchor and missed the dogs.

I didn't sleep much that night, dreaming awake, dreaming asleep.

At our arraignment the following day, guards brought us through a tunnel to a close gray room with shedding paint and a ceiling with several fallen tiles, allowing a peek to the tangle of rusted pipes above. Iron bars formed one entire wall, as in a cage. Beyond the bars were two desks, two manual typewriters, a French man who I knew as a translator, and two clerks. They were to read the accusations and we were to respond. That is what we knew from the five-minute brief from Russell's lawyer, who had been quickly drafted into the role of our defense. Minutes before the proceedings our counsel instructed us to listen, and respond. Nothing more.

Then the fiction unfolded.

From the fat file, inches thick with documents, testimonies, eyewitness accounts sewn together with thick twine, emerged a tale of three violent people—us.

One evening in early May, witnesses observed as we guided a mid-sized truck onto the property, and with sinister intent unloaded tables and chairs. We were taking over. Staking claim. Moving in. The witness who had seen us—who said she did not dare stop us for fear of how we might react—was a woman we knew. The university used to send a representative periodically to check if Russell was still breathing. "What a beautiful afternoon" and "Gee, it looks like Lobo will never leave from underneath that blooming jasmine." She wasn't fond of us, and we couldn't tell why, but that held little importance as long as she treated Russell kindly.

I suddenly remembered the phone call she made several months prior to ask for the spelling of my full name. I thought she must keep thorough records. "S as in Samuel... A... N as in Nancy..." I enunciated clearly and thanked her for calling.

But when... when had a truck appeared on the property that could have been mistaken for this conspiratorial truck? I reached for some memory of behavior that could be misconstrued as menacing, some furniture that might have been improperly delivered. John stopped me.

"Whoa, whoa, whoa! This is no mistaken impression, man. It's a colossal fabrication. Somebody cooked this up on purpose."

Whoa.

It wasn't clear though, for what purpose. Why us, why the story, why jail. Oddly, the outlandish story gave me hope. If the university had a legitimate case or some tiny loophole—a legal reason for claiming the land—they wouldn't have had to resort to lies. Lies should be easy to disprove. But where this left us at the moment was clear. On the wrong side of the gate. Like Lobo asleep under the jasmine, we had settled in and taken possession at Casa Ames. And apparently the university had had enough.

Then, as instructed by our lawyer, we responded. Confident of our words, our voices trembled from not having slept or eaten. But we trusted the buoyancy of our truth.

"We are Russell's friends and were invited to share his home since..."

We each told our story. The whole procedure took several hours and long before we finished, our lawyer had left. His assistant notified us that we would remain in custody, sleeping on the floor, for six nights while they worked on our defense.

Six nights. Nearly a week. We wouldn't get out till Sunday. Mexican law at that time did not operate under an assumption of innocence, and allowed six days for a defendant to prove innocence before continuing with the order to incarcerate, the *auto de formal prision*. Our innocence was obvious—why did they need six days? Russell could explain in four words. "They are my friends."

Beth pushed us a bag with turkey sandwiches from the other side of the bars. With a blue felt tip pen lent to us by the guard, we wrote our first notes home on the paper napkins inside the lunch bag. To Bill. To my sister. To John's kids.

Re: A Short Absence.

From the Oaxaca State Penitentiary at Ixcotel. Seems there was a misunderstanding about Russell's land...

We asked the assistant if the lawyer could come to the prison to talk with us in the afternoon. We wanted to know how this would proceed, understand the steps.

We awaited the lawyer as friends filed in to bring hugs, soap, shampoo, toothpaste, toothbrush, books, news of Russell, paper and pens. And deodorant and fresh clothes enough for six days. We had the tools and the parts—we lacked the instruction manual. The lawyer didn't show.

The suite of unfurnished offices where they held us had three rooms. John and I each had a room of our own, leaving one office "for official use only." We had a bathroom and a shower plus a reception area with a table. Joe spent days with us until 8 pm when they escorted him to the infirmary to sleep. This is where he spent the rest of his prison time. The third office was used occasionally to fingerprint newly arrived prisoners.

"What did you guys do to score these good rooms?" they'd ask.

"Nothing."

"Yeah, me neither."

As far as I could tell, the other prisoners in holding were shoved together in stone bunks in a tight gray room, just next to ours. Our rooms had doors that we could close to sit alone and read. Write. Think. Stare at our watches. No clock hung on the wall.

During the ensuing days we worked out a list of witnesses that could vouch for us and waited to talk to the lawyer. But the lawyer never showed. Nobody asked for our input.

The Consular Agent visited.

"Please ask your sister to stop having your friends send faxes to ask for your release. They tie up the fax machine and waste our paper."

"I can't call my sister. We don't have phone privileges."

"I'll see what I can do."

Within these first few days, my sister had mobilized hundreds of people from my e-mail address book. I hadn't known. Bill put up a website and called reporters. Friends contacted members of Congress and Senators throughout the United States. We knew that outside a movement had already begun to pulsate for our release. Yet inside, we were helpless—we hadn't heard from our lawyer since the day of our incarceration. The resulting impotence lay prickly and atomic inside us, a scream swallowed, an explosion about to burst.

"What do you need?" The Consular Agent visited again and expected us to request pillows or aspirin.

"The lawyer. We need the lawyer."

"Oh, I met with him today. Don't worry. He is doing everything possible."

Everything possible. I pictured a grim-faced doctor peeling off blue latex gloves and shaking his head. Friends had told us that the lawyer was busy answering to Tony, who was taking out legal protections of his own so that he and his Bed and Breakfast staff were protected from possible future arrests. We were told that in a meeting of the neighbors who pulled together behind the cause, Tony and the Consular Agent complained that we were whining and needed too much hand-holding. We were told, also, that friends stood up to remind them that we were sleeping on the floor. And that we were innocent. And obviously not being heard. They countered that simple information is not hand holding and far from being whiners, we were holding up well considering the lack of information, as Tony would know if he dared to visit. We were told that there was a rift forming among the neighbors, a fault line drawn at the doors of the Bed and Breakfast. The neighbors were pulling away from Tony.

We played cards. Read. Thought. Stared at our watches. So many friends visited. The nuns from the children's shelter. Friends from Mexico City and others who brought bagels or anthologies of short stories or floral-scented body lotion. Visitors had to wait in a long line each day, as their bags were examined for contraband fruit or lipstick. We wrote more notes home, and friends turned scribes sent them daily. Our fierce, protective herd. Friends were our oxygen, our nutrients, our shut-eye, our grace. In the gloom and uncertainty that surrounded us daily, in the absence of clarity, they were always there. In person, through notes, on the other end of the phone. Because of friends, we did not drown, as the water lapped at our chins.

The lawyer absent, we were told to trust that he and the other men affecting the case on the outside had our best interests at heart, that they were moving heaven and earth. Our heavens and earths had already moved. We wanted no more of that—we wanted answers. But we were expected to wait and trust patiently by day, sleep soundly in sweet confidence on the floor at night—innocent and deprived of liberty. I was unaccustomed to dependency. To be inactive and out of contact while allegedly capable men, some of whom I barely knew, assumed control of our lives without consultation with us, was possible only at the cost of that same trust that was supposed to buoy us. I developed an inconsolable cough at night, where I would bark like a chained dog, keeping John awake and waking hoarse by morning.

The guards let us know when we were allowed to make calls. Twice a day with lines so long you would have thought the secret to eternal youth was at the other end. But it was only a voice. Of a grandmother. A teacher. A lover. A priest. Of a lawyer's secretary.

"I'm sorry. The attorney is out. May I take a message?"

"Please tell him it is Mary Ellen in the Ixcotel State Penitentiary, and we are still waiting to see him. It has been three days. Please tell him that I want to talk to the judge."

"Mary Ellen. Two words?"

"How about I speak to his assistant."

She put me on with the assistant and I begged. I tried to make him promise me the lawyer would come. I asked him if this was usual for people represented not to see their lawyer. He said don't worry, don't worry.

"I'm not worried. I am angry. We are alone here."

"I'll let him know," he said.

I knew I had the right to see the judge—and for her to see me, a person, not merely a name with a case number on a page in a file in a stack on a desk in an office. I didn't know what I would say, but I trusted what was left to trust—myself. I thought that she would hear me, grab the truth and let the swirling mess of lies zing into orbit.

Wednesday night, the third night on the floor, I lay down coughing. Even at 9pm, I thought the lawyer might still show. It's crazy. "Anything is possible" was branded into our daily existence. The bad anythings, and the good anythings. We might be innocently sentenced to prison. And the lawyer might show at 9pm. He didn't, and some of the only tears I knew in Ixcotel, were tears that night of impotence: of having so much to say, and nobody to say it to, of wanting so much to hear about what was happening, because surely things were happening, and instead being patted on the head and told to trust, there there now, don't you worry. In the world that still made sense to me, I knew how to help myself. That world swirled to nearly dark, to a mere pinhole of light. I coughed as loud as I could, great spasms of coughs mixed with tears that wouldn't quite dissolve the mess of emotions in my chest, and wouldn't quite bring the lawyer.

Late on Thursday, he arrived in a rush and without our file. Halfway into the six days that would define our freedom.

"Do you have your witnesses for the testimonies tomorrow?"

"What witnesses? What testimony?"

"Oh, they didn't tell you?"

"No, *they* didn't. We expected to see you before this."

"I've been busy doing everything possible."

The testimonies the next day didn't happen, even though we managed to assemble a few witnesses through the message vine. The translator hadn't been called. This was the lawyer's responsibility. When a translator arrived, the court did not approve him.

On Friday, the lawyer stomped in, choleric. We called his office too often. This was an insult. He took no responsibility for our eroded trust.

"I have been a Doctor of Law for twenty five years. How dare you doubt me!"

"That you are doing *something* is clear. We just don't know *what*. Can you explain the steps so we understand what 'everything possible' includes?" My desperation was evident, but I distilled every possible ion of control to remain focused. I still wanted to see the judge, and I needed him for that.

I experienced Hurricane Gilbert as a Resort Representative in Cancún in 1988. The strongest hurricane of that century, with winds over 185 miles per hour. After the storm passed, our work began in earnest to evacuate. I escorted a bus with fifty clients over a highway strewn with palm leaves and bits of reed homes, for five hours to Merida where a plane awaited. When we arrived, I was called to the control tower where a crackly phone call had come through from our home office. They had not been in touch with any of us since the storm made landfall. After shouts of "*hallelujah*" from the team up north, we devised a plan for more evacuations. They asked me how I could appear so calm. "Thankfully, I have work to do." When my work was done, when a rescue plane took us from Cancún to Toronto, then, I liquefied.

So I did not scream at this pathetic man. I did not cry. For a day and a half longer we needed him. We had work to do.

"And you may remember I requested a visit with the judge."

"What will you say to her? She won't listen to you. Let me handle it."

"I need to do what is in my power to help myself. I am asking you to do your part to get me that audience with the judge. Whether she listens or not—I want to speak with her."

"I'm through with this. I've done all I can." If he could have slammed a door on the way out, he would have.

Day six, 4pm. On Sunday, the guards ordered me to the judge's quarters.

The judge was about my age. Though I suspected she had been "bought" by the university, I thought that she would detect my transparency. That she would make the right choice. By this time, the rage I had carefully swallowed for six days had stolen my voice. I could barely squeak out words.

"We have not had an opportunity to refute all that the university alleges."

"You have had the time allowed by law."

"I am not certain our lawyer has done everything possible."

"You may be right. This case is much more complex than you know. Interests exist that you may be unaware of. People should have negotiated differently to end this, long long ago. I am sorry. But I will do what is possible from my end."

Day six, 6 pm. The judge's clerk arrived with the papers.

Auto de formal prisión.

John, Joe and I looked at each other, and signed silently in triplicate. What was left to do? We were presumed to be guilty of the concocted crimes, and not having been able to prove our innocence, we would be going on to the real jail with the real criminals, the general populace.

On Monday, October 13, 2003, we awoke as every day—at 6 am to sweep and mop our quarters. Roll call at 7 am. I was alone on the line in the holding area that Monday. Women are usually gone after a night or two—prostitutes get bailed out by someone who cares about them. Others, for lack of lawyer, enter the main compound after three days. Several of my former line-mates had already been moved inside.

We had informed friends that we wanted a new lawyer, and had interviewed three that morning. The first two were unconvincing, and we waited for the third, recommended by the women's shelter where I volunteered.

From the table where I sat in our quarters, I saw a well-dressed, handsome man come through the entry gates. He walked with authority and confidence. I wished he were a lawyer. I wished he were coming to see us, but he walked right past us. Thirty minutes later he returned and introduced himself. He had been sent by the women's shelter. Tomás had gone to research the case with his contacts. The interview shifted quickly into action plan, as he anticipated our questions, explained legal terminology and identified possibilities for recourse. He explained the case's unconstitutionality, and on those grounds alone we could act. It could take several months, but a strong case could be litigated against the university.

"And you have so many on your side. I heard your former employer has stepped in. They called the Department of Tourism in Mexico City—that's a good, strong move. And you must have more relationships we can use. I'm a champion chess player. We'll work together on this."

The magic words.

"In cases like these, the course of action can change quickly. Options are plentiful when innocence is so clear. We need to have good communication. I will be in Ixcotel nearly every day."

As if he knew.

The guards came for John first. Though he didn't show much emotion—it was his style—I worried. He spoke some Spanish, but maybe not enough to stare down the toughies.

"How bad are they inside?"

"They are calm right now."

Were the women still calm, these six days later?

My Mexican friends used to joke: "The stork made a mistake when it delivered you in *el norte*. Danged bird should have left you in Mexico with us." Part of what I loved about Mexico's effect on me was finding my way despite my differences. Blurring the border. I had lived in cities, in resorts, towns, villages and among indigenous and farmers. At every step I had been accepted—for speaking the language, for knowing about autonomy, soap operas, song lyrics and ingredients for *mole*. I knew some slang, some swear words, some dates in history. I wasn't Mexican—you noticed from leagues away. Blonde and blue-eyed, I hid a dark Latina streak. Would these prisoners want to crack the marble to assure the vein was authentic? A lifetime in tourism had taught me to relate to all kinds of people, but I had no experience with criminals. I feared losing my balance.

For seventeen years in Mexico I studied the lives and landscapes around me because I desired—more than anything—to do the work of fitting in. I assimilated Mexico's complex grammar, becoming comfortable with the uncertainty of her subjunctive mood – a language that hinted at her transitory nature. *Ser* and *Estar*. "To be" and "to be—for now." I knew about the fault lines. How everything could change in a day. I knew the dance.

And during six excruciating days in Ixcotel I believed that fortune would allow me to slip through the bars. For the first time in Mexico I realized that more than anything I did not want to be—please—not like them.

Ahora sí. I would see them on the inside.

Blackbirds in the Pomegranate Tree

BERTA

Berta was one of the few women small enough to fit under the single set of bunks in our sleeping quarters. That's the only way everyone would fit—with Berta under the bed and Susa's legs under the shelving unit where we stored our bedding. I never figured out what kind of seniority gave bunk privileges, but there were two stacked mattresses for four women, the only real bedding in our quarters. From my first night in the compound, Berta and I saw eye to eye at bedtime. Literally. From her protected space under the bunk, she tut-tutted as the rest of us scooted like tiles in a sliding puzzle across the floor. The space assigned to me by the boss lady was alongside Berta, close as if we were sharing a sleeping bag.

"Better unwrap 'em now."

Berta spied the four cough drops I placed beside the rolled up sweater I used as a pillow. My cough had not let up. It came on without warning and I feared how the women would react if I choked my way through my first night in.

"Nobody likes rustling in the middle of the night. Unwrap 'em now. The rats don't like menthol. And you better keep a roll of toilet paper close. That's how we do it here. There's no paper in the john."

She announced to the women before the lights went out that first night, that she might just wake up speaking English. I didn't know enough about Berta yet to know she was just doing what was expected of her. Berta made them laugh. She winked at me and pulled her blankets up over her head.

I slept—that night and always—with my pen and notebook under my head, afraid that if we separated, I might understand even less. Mercifully, the four unwrapped cough drops kept my throat soothed enough and if anyone awoke in the night, it wasn't the fault of my cough.

Berta slept under a bed. In this corner of Ixcotel State Penitentiary called the *cacahuate*—the peanut, in allusion to its size—forty-five women patchworked themselves into their tightly choreographed spaces on the cement floor, breath to breath, ragged foot to weary head. A little known wildlife fact that I've carried around with me since I was a teen: twenty-one newborn possums can fit into a matchbox. I read it as a space-filler in the Schenectady Gazette in the days before computers perfected page layout. I couldn't picture it—*twenty-one possums? How?* That night, the dense weave of women in the *cacahuate* opened a me-sized space for one more; in tangible portrayal of just how small we can become. The room pretended darkness, but the spotlight from the guard tower oozed through the broken windows into the stony gray of the room. Wedged into this family of cocooned women, I felt the floor press up beneath me with a cold concrete reminder that we had few choices now. I had slept on floors and rocky earth before—by choice. In that choosing lay the comfort.

Berta didn't seem to mind her space under the bed. She said she could dream there of home, without the fear of having the Holy Mary squashed out of her as somebody stumbled toward the door. The boss lady put the crack addicts and night pee-ers together at the exit, but often someone would unroll in the middle of the night to pick across the dark mosaic of snoring woman-mounds to get outside. Maybe they just wanted to make sure the moon was still hanging in the sky. Maybe they needed to stretch. Maybe they tired of hearing Berta dream of home. She snuffled in her sleep when she dreamed of home.

Berta's attempts to make us laugh were heroic given the setting. She rarely missed a chance. On the nine o'clock television soap, a young, overdressed starlet whimpered to her unnaturally red-headed friend:

"I don't know what to do! I'm pregnant. But I don't know who my baby's father is!"

Berta cackled.

"She should have opened her eyes when they did it! Then she would know!" And the women of Ixcotel laughed. At Berta—and at the stupidity of the woman who hadn't opened her eyes.

The guards came to call roll four times a day. It was the only time the male guards were inside our area, unless there was a theft, or an escapee on the roof. One hundred and ten women assembled according to arrival date as we waited to hear our names. "Mari" they called me, shortening my name as if I were a friend. "*Presente.*" Lest we forget, they made us say, four times a day, "I am here." Berta got a "doña" in front of her name. She inspired respect. Roll call was a nuisance, but a break from the monotony, just something to do. The women covered their mischievous smiles with work-worn hands as Berta whispered.

"Look at him. He thinks he's so cool and his sunglasses are on crooked."

"You think El Ché ever changes his socks? Something smells like rotten mangoes."

"Hey, Concha! Get any lately?"

The women of Ixcotel laughed, their smiles laced with gaps and gold.

One afternoon in the tattered shade of the only tree in the women's courtyard, a sprawling pomegranate, Berta sat with her feet propped up on a red bucket, sewing. She told me her story of how she landed in Ixcotel. Everybody had a story. Not everyone was willing to tell it. Both innocent and guilty women were ashamed—for being tricked or for being caught. On that day, writing next to Berta as she sewed, I let out a sigh at the right time, and she said, "I remember too."

Berta had been collecting sticks for kitchen firewood on her last afternoon of freedom with her two children. Bundling the dry branches on her slight back with an old shawl, she headed down from the hillside with Ana and Francisco.

Francisco complained. "I wish we had a burro like Señor López has, so we wouldn't have to carry everything on our backs."

"You wish we had a burro? If you're wishing for things we'll never have, why not wish *big*, for a house in the city and a maid who will cook for us?" Berta laughed.

"I like our house, mamá," Ana piped up.

"Here. Give me your sticks. You two keep wishing for a burro." She clucked and shook her head and pushed them to walk on. While uphill still some distance from her home, she saw a car below and two men pushing her husband around.

"Let´s run. Your papá is in trouble."

They scampered down the steep slope, and sticks fell from Berta's bundle. Ana wanted to gather them.

"No, no! Leave them! We'll come back!" she yelled to her children. As they arrived the men pinned Noé's hands behind his back and pushed him toward the car.

"What are you doing to my husband? Where are you taking him?"

"He's your husband?"

Berta nodded. They had these two skinny children together. And he was a good father to the three older children of the men who had come before him.

"Yes, I told you that. Tell me what you are doing with him!" Assuming no wrongdoing on her husband's part, she didn't ask what he had done.

"You know, then, what he does in the fields..."

With one hairy arm the man made an arc that seemed to take in the entire state.

"Yes. He tends Señor Pinal's sorghum, so? What do you want?"

"We'll let the judge answer that. He's got questions for you both."

Berta noticed that he had a crooked nose, as if he had once been punched hard in a fight over a woman or a horse.

Berta and the children went with the men and with Noé, in the back of the black car. She wondered about the questions. Noé was a farmer. What mystery lay in that? All she knew was that she packed his tortillas in the morning, and he left early after two cups of strong coffee. He came home at the end of the day tired and smelling of earth. She sometimes rubbed corn oil into his callused hands. He never thanked her, and never hit her. What was there to tell?

"Married, Gringa?"

"No..."

"Me neither. Not to Noé, and not to the others. I never wanted to mess with papers and officials and stuff, and now look at me! But Noé, he's a good man. I didn't know where we were going when I met him, but wherever it was I wanted to go with him. Is this it? Is this where we were going?"

Berta looked off, as if into the distance, though she could only see to the opposite wall. She continued her story.

The children watched silently as their home disappeared. They had never been in a car. Berta stared at the dirt on the men's collars and thought about how late she'd be making dinner. She was hungry. Noé bit into his fist.

"Ay, *mi gordo*. Did something happen today in your field?"

"Shhh… Nothing. Nothing happened. I earned my *pesos* like always."

Berta searched his eyes. She was suddenly scared of what she didn't know. Noé seemed scared of what he did know. He had been with the police before. He had even been in jail.

In the end, there were no questions. Noé was jailed on a suspicion, and Berta was brought in on an ugly man's whim. Guilty of a crime in a field she had never seen. These things happen, she had heard. In the municipal headquarters, Ana and Francisco witnessed the body searches and the photos, and saw the police chief spit on the ground when Noé explained how he spent twelve hours a day in Señor Pinal's six hectares, keeping the weeds from his sorghum. "Even an *indio* knows marijuana, *cabrón*." The children stayed in the headquarters behind bars with Noé and Berta for four hours. The officials had allowed Berta to send a note to Señora Elvia, the neighbor, to come for them.

"We'll go pick up the sticks, mamá."

And Berta kissed them and told them she would be home soon, and not to give much fuss to Señora Elvia.

"Have kids, Gringa?"

"No…"

"Sometimes in here, I wish I didn't. I don't know if it's harder to imagine them crying for me, or imagine them happy without me."

She reached into the pocket of her cotton skirt, where she had a worn card imprinted with a prayer and an image of the *Virgen de Juquila*, a *virgen morenita* with skin the color of Oaxacan earth.

Blessed Mother, Virgin of Hope, we ask for forgiveness from our sins for they are many. Deliver us from all suffering. If the world brings us injustice, misery and sin, and you see that our lives are afflicted, do not abandon us.

"It says here "if." *If* there is injustice. *If* there is misery. Who wrote this? A blind man?"

Berta's cynicism shifted quickly to hope.

"This *Virgen*, she helps me. She's a smart one—knows what it's like to miss a child. I ask her to take care of them for me. But this, now *this* is my prize."

From the other pocket she removed and unfolded a well-creased drawing from Francisco. A jacaranda tree in full purple bloom, outside a home that was taller than the tree. Wisps of birds tickled his bright blue sky, and a family smiled.

Berta and Noé were taken away from their remote town because crimes like theirs were too important for the municipal jail that housed drunks and men avoiding their duty to fight fires or repair the roads. They were taken in a closed truck with no windows, which seemed to stop a hundred times between their earth and the sprawling compound where they landed. Along the way they picked up men and women who spoke Zapotec, Mixtec, Mixe, Chatino. Berta and Noé were able to understand some words in Mixe. "They hit me hard with a big stick," an older woman with a long ebony-gray braid said as she pointed to her knees. Maybe that's what she said. Or maybe she didn't. Berta decided not to listen and just sat with her hands in her lap, picking the day's dirt from underneath her fingernails, reciting memorized verses from the Bible, and wondering how she got this far from home.

The court appointed her a representative who was young and tired beyond his years.

"Don't worry. We have lots of these cases. We'll get it straightened out. How much money do you have?"

And Berta heard words like *writ* and *appeal* and *bail* and *bribe*, but didn't quite understand how any of them would get her back washing clothes for her children. She couldn't read or write, and x'd the papers as her representative indicated, right before he disappeared. When she asked the social worker about him, she was told only that he was reassigned. "These things happen, Berta."

"Have a lawyer, Gringa?"

"Yes..."

"Good. I hope he wears nice leather shoes. Mine wore sneakers. The better to run away with."

And Berta gave a hearty laugh and rolled her eyes up toward the sky leaking through the pomegranate leaves.

At three thirty, the women signed up for the afternoon visit with the men. Berta was usually the first to sign, but the line of regulars was long. There are one hundred and ten incarcerated women, and twelve hundred men. The four o'clock visits, every day but Sunday, were the highlights of many people's days. Our only consistent daily exercise was walking those seven minutes to the men's courtyard, where the women spent twenty supervised and carefully counted minutes visiting through the metal bars. The women and men slipped hands through the bars, met lips in between, or exchanged notes or little gifts of pumpkin seeds or potato chips. I went to see John to mull together the latest word from the lawyer, or share news clippings on the case, brought in by friends. Flor put on pearly lipstick and pink high heels to see a man accused of car theft that she met at the Independence Day dance. Berta went to see Noé in her blue cardigan and flip flops. They talked of the children, and Berta laughed and tousled Noé's head. They shared the drawing from Francisco. Berta gave the flattened page to Noé on Mondays, Wednesdays and Fridays, and he gave it back on Tuesdays, Thursdays and Saturdays. Berta kept it on Sunday, and didn't share her wise *Virgen* on any day.

At four-twenty, the guards led the women back and Berta hurried off to return to her space under the pomegranate tree to sit in her sewing circle. She was working on a huge white napkin that would keep her family's tortillas warm. In the waning light of the afternoon, she stitched with her head down, a short, curly gray cloud hovering over her work. She placed the needle close to the last crimson thread pulled tightly across the stretched cotton, humming something that sounded like a hymn. I watched her and imagined memories of her children wound around her fingers with each thread. Her still-life garden had vivid daisies speckled by a few tiny drops of blood. Sometimes the needle slipped and brought her pain to the surface. She must be remembering her children. Right now, Berta was far from laughter. We sat quietly around her, sewing, writing, remembering as a group.

On Mondays the Christians brought tamales and Bibles. Berta sat with them for two hours while they prayed for strength and solace for these women who were already stronger than the Christian matrons in their bright floral dresses could possibly imagine. Berta helped to arrange the plastic chairs in a circle around the prayer leaders, and invited newly-arrived women to join. Against the background of salsa music from a tinny radio, shouts from the women at the laundry sinks and Susa hawking her shoeshine, Berta and the Christian women held their hands high to the heavens, shouting "amen" and repeating again and again the words they knew by heart. Berta was sure about her Bible. She adored her *Virgen* who watched out for "if." She was devoted to her Mondays and the circle of white plastic chairs, and passed out tamales to the women who attended, though she ate none herself. She didn't have much appetite without the kids to cook for. She told me eye to eye before sleep one night, that she wasn't sure about heaven anymore. She said she sometimes lay awake with her eyes squeezed tight, remembering the prickles of light in her night sky at home. She peeked once, and the mattress was still overhead.

Day of the Dead was Berta's holiday. A feast of laughter, of dancing devils and teasing skeletons. A celebration of the inevitable, with golden flowers and ornate altars to honor the departed. There was to be a contest for the finest altar—the warden promised one pair of new sneakers to the winning section. Family members brought everything they could for the decoration, and the prison took up a collection of spare coins to provide the materials for the altars. Fifty cents here and there bought fruit and leafy bamboo-like stalks for the arch. Our altar came alive with oranges and apples and *jicama* and *tejocotes*. The marigold blooms were like incense, fragrant and ablaze. With hands that had inherited centuries of knowing how to make the best of what little they had, the women arranged sugar skulls, amaranth cakes, fat loaves of bread and pictures of soldier fathers, baby brothers and sister brides deceased. The candles were lit, and night duty rotation was set up to make sure that nothing caught fire and the rats didn't steal the bread. The boss lady said the fruit would be distributed to everybody when the altar was taken down. Berta was anxious for an apple, even though these looked harder than the ones she used to cut up for the children for breakfast.

"Even the apples are hard in here. Everything is hard in here. Speaking of hard, hey ladies—is it four o'clock yet?"

And Berta laughed again, to nobody in particular.

On the night of the festivities, doña Flor put on a play with the theater group. We walked en masse to the men's side where a stage had been constructed. The fiesta had the air of a community social—there in the men's courtyard surrounded by boxing rings and basketball hoops—except everyone there was missing their own community. The play was about a peasant man whose only wish in life was to eat an entire turkey. Berta thought him frivolous, and only watched to see doña Flor play the part of Death. Her Death was imposing but frolicsome. She wore black robes with a bright sash of yellow and pink psychedelic flowers. When Flor laughed in her role as Death, her laughter welled up, full and dark, from that same spring where tears are born.

"You do not... understand... the gift I gave you."

At the end, we clapped and whistled as Flor took her bow on the plywood stage under the lights from the guard tower. She wasn't the star, but she was the one we wanted to see.

Afterwards prisoners danced to a brass band. Everyone danced with a devil or death, a whimsical death, a playful death. A death with mirrors to scare away vultures, or a long tail to trail back to the world of the living. These invented deaths helped some feel more in control of their fate. "Death! I paint you in spirited colors. You are frisky tonight. I am not afraid."

The musicians played all night, raucous and rhythmic, dressed as devils and whores. Many men wore disguises, though the women went as themselves. The buxom bride and the groom, the nurse and the old lady were men underneath the wigs and blue eye shadow. Berta giggled at how they teetered in heels. To me the masks were disconcerting. Too many layers, masks on masks. Sunlight allowed me to recognize the ones we wore by day: today I am a teacher, today I am strong. But in the glare of the spotlights from the towers, these masks did not have the same subtlety of pretense. I watched, wary, from the bleachers where the families gathered, to avoid the invitations to dance that came from slack-jawed demons and hairy-legged nurses. I left early to keep my post at the altar. I didn't understand all of what I witnessed in front of the altar that night, until I chatted with Berta the next day.

Just before 4pm and Berta and I were under the pomegranate tree. She hadn't signed on to the visitation list.

"*Gringa*, you went home early last night."

"Yeah, I didn't like the masks. I couldn't recognize anyone."

"That's how it's supposed to be. You don't recognize anyone *without* their mask either!"

Berta continued, telling me the story of what happened after I left.

Berta and Noé danced, too, spinning in the delirious crowd. Berta spun so much she couldn't quite tell which side of death she was on.

"Where are we, Noé?"

He had no response.

"I think you knew all along about that field."

"Ay, what a stupid woman! Where do you think I got money for the refrigerator with a light inside?"

"But you said you wouldn't do that again! I trusted you! The children… Now look! We are so far from them and who cares about a light bulb in an empty refrigerator?"

"Ay, what a stupid woman…"

She wanted to run back to her shrouded space under the bed where she wouldn't be trampled. She wanted to hit him. But he had never hit her and she wouldn't raise the first fist. It was Thursday and Noé hadn't given her their son's drawing yet. Before heading for the gate, Berta asked him for it.

"Ay, Berta. I was hoping you wouldn't ask. He can do another one."

Berta's face was stricken.

"What do you mean?"

"I forgot to take it out of my pocket when I scrubbed my jeans today, so I threw it away. It was torn and soppy. These things happen. I'll get Francisco to draw you another."

Berta slapped Noé hard on his cheek and ran and ran away from him, until the guards stopped her.

"Hey! No running! And skinny as you are you won't get far from us anyway."

The guards shouted, and their laughter and the brass trumpets filled Berta's ears as she blinked back tears.

Berta's version of the story ended with her cursing the guards who followed her back to the compound, and going to her space under the bed to sleep, lamenting ever having met such a stupid man, who can't even wash a pair of jeans without messing up.

But I know that Berta first peeked in at the candles. I was squinting at the candlelight on the altar making star patterns in the golden dark when I saw her enter. She was crying. Our heroic well of laughter was shaking with sobs. There are times when the pain inside and the pain outside cannot be kept apart by a mere sheath of skin. She stood in front of the flickering altar, and approached the sugar skulls where sequined eyes winked back amidst the candles.

"Ay. What a stupid woman!"

And I saw her dig her hand into the pocket where I knew she kept her most precious possession, and watched her as she tore it into a pile of confetti that she let flutter to the dirt floor before the altar.

"Stupid, stupid woman! You promised!"

Berta wiped the tears from her face with the sleeve of her blouse, quieted herself, and grabbed a hard apple from the altar before returning to the *cacahuate*, where she picked across a field of snoring women who had already given up on laughter and death for the night, to squirm into the safe space underneath the bed.

After she left, I went to gather the pieces of the picture that Berta had torn apart, expecting to find bits of her jacaranda tree and happy birds, but I found only the pieces of her *Virgen's* once-flowing mantle, her prayer now jagged and broken.

"Stupid, stupid woman…"

Berta's cry entered on a rush of breeze that ruffled the flames.

The women of Ixcotel laugh when the blackbirds chatter atop the pomegranate tree. They say the birds get excited when somebody is getting out.

"Look at them. They are all aflutter again! I wonder who'll get out today?"

Soraya mused as she pulled her crochet hook through glittering silver yarn, looking up through the branches toward the quiver of wings.

Berta's laugh was diluted. She shook her head.

"Funny how we come back to sit here every day, every identical day after day—with those identical birds up there shitting on our identical stupid heads. Funny, isn't it?"

And the women nodded and hmmmm'ed and kept on with their needles.

"God willing, those birds will flap for me soon. I'm tired of this."

Berta put her napkin back into her sewing basket and stored the needle freshly threaded with a brilliant green. It was Monday and the gospel circle would arrive soon. She stood to set up the ring of white plastic chairs.

-godwilling-godwilling-godwilling-godwilling-

The birds intoned from the topmost branches of the pomegranate, and a few, impatient for change, took off for the mountains that only they could see.

CASE NOTES I

That same day I joined the women in their compound, Tomas arrived for his first visit.

"Did you know about the arrangement with the previous lawyer?"

"What arrangement?"

"With the land."

"No, Tomas, I wasn't involved in any of that. What do you mean?"

"Seems there was an agreement with the civil case, that the lawyer was to be paid in part by receiving some of Mr. Ames' land. And the consular agent is included in any potential distribution, too."

Speechless, I grit my teeth and took stock. The first lawyer visited once during those first six days, and only after we begged. The consular agent assured us that he and Tony were "taking care of everything" on the outside. Their "everything" didn't seem to be the same as our "everything." On our own we wrote notes and lists and whole monologues that we thought would prove our innocence. But nobody asked for them, and they remained as space-fillers, just another invented game that prisoners play to pass the time. It seemed suddenly, that on the outside people did not want to make a move that might put the land at risk. Perhaps our release was a second priority?

"Did you understand what I said?" Tomas saw the strained look on my face.

"Yes, I understood the words. And maybe I understand a lot more now."

The land "belonged" to the university since the arrangement the Ames' made in the 80s. Now these men – Tony, the consular agent and the lawyer – seemed intent on trying to wrestle it back. It felt to me at that moment, that it was their very personal interest in this land with disputed title that kept me on a cold floor to sleep and within these gray walls, innocent.

The judge's words which seemed cryptic at the time were now painfully decipherable:

"There are interests of which you may be unaware."

A day or two after I entered the women's compound, I was told I had a visit from my cousin. Blonde like me, I guess we could have been related. The guards were not convinced and didn't let him enter, perhaps because of the quizzical look on my face when my cousin was announced. I have none.

Kevin was a reporter from the Washington Post. He shook my hand through the bars between the courtyard and the corridor where he stood. After he identified himself, the first thing he said was "Who is Bill? You owe him big!" Bill had tracked down a Pulitzer-prize-winning journalist from the Washington Post who had done extensive research and reporting on crime and punishment in Mexico. Kevin knew his way around the jails of Mexico and wasted no time getting to Ixcotel.

On October 18, five days after I ate my first lunch with the women of Ixcotel, the Washington Post printed over a thousand words in section A, with pictures, under the title "Three Americans

Jailed in Bizarre Mexican Land Dispute; Caretakers of Man, 91, Held in Standoff Involving a Member of President Fox's Cabinet."

Oh, yes. I neglected to mention. The rector of the university also just happened to be the Chief of Mexico's Federal Police.

Complicated. Scary.

More words from the judge made sense.

"This case is much more complex than you know."

I felt very small next to these men, this greed, this complexity.

SORAYA

Don Temo watched the sun as it stretched out of its mountain cradle on the day his mystery was born. In his language, minutely aware of the changing earth and heavens, that sun was called *the star that dawns when the day is long*. But not everything can be expressed in language, rich as his was. For greater mysteries, don Temo had his weaving.

I met don Temo through his rugs when I was guiding the group of poets through the craft villages around Oaxaca. Don Temo gave us demonstrations of how wool, shaved from the back of sheep crusted in dung, was transformed into colorful geometric interpretations of his mysteries. He told us that some weavers wove circles, jaguars, jagged diamond patterns. They were attractive rugs, but don Temo considered the best work to be the weaving that interpreted intangible truths that defied expression through words. His variations of pigment and intertwining yarns could convey mysteries, though, he admitted, they could not explain them.

He took us on a tour of his vats of stewing wool, his looms that had translated hundreds of mysteries and his collection of flowers, rock and bark he used for dye. He was an alchemist, born knowing how to produce colors and give them a voice. His life close to the earth had given him a particular facility for expressing the essence of a pine, its growth and sturdy bearing, with just the right spiral of green from carefully fermented alfalfa, or the trust of good earth with a swipe of root-darkened brown. The intricate geometrics of his rugs held his whole cosmology. He could dye wool to reflect the exact shade of a waning autumn moon. For a spring moon, for hope, he added more marigold petals. The downy white *cochinilla* bug that grew on cactus paddles had rich wine guts that gave him red for wildflowers, and for expressions of love or grief. The same dye, worked with a delicate hand, would give him the suffused lavender of a storm-kissed sky, or of futures foretold.

We chatted as the poets went off to look for rugs to take home.

"Once, so many dawns ago, I was spellbound by a sight not even my rugs could capture. I could not imagine how to reproduce in wools, the wonderment of seeing my newborn daughter's squirming pink tongue. Her tongue! Or the rich brown tuft of hair on her head that fit into the palm of my hand."

That day, he held her warm, wriggling body to his heart, and even with his years of watching and translating his ephemeral earth and sky, his head spun around those changes that arose in the space of one sunrise: a daughter, inexpressible in wool or words.

He showed me a rug displayed behind Plexiglas on the cracked mint green wall of his studio, while the poets unrolled lesser rugs in the patio.

"As close as I could come."

This rug was not rectangular, it was an octagon. Don Temo had to build a special loom to produce the rug, and completed it in three years. A ruby sunburst slightly off center was the result of a precise stewing of his finest combed lamb's wool in the *cochinilla* pot, then drying it on a perfectly sunless day. It was surrounded by icy blue mosaic waves, reminiscent of the fine work I had seen on the temples at Mitla. Don Temo called his work a fluid-sounding word in Zapotec that he said meant "when bewilderment lands on your shoulder."

"An anthropologist from your country passed through here once. He was interested in my colors. He told me that ancient cultures named all other colors before they named blue. *Azul.* It is mystery. The heavens are blue. I am told the deep sea is blue. Like our mountains at dusk."

"My daughter is now grown. Oh, but she is still a mystery! That young woman has shown me that I understand absolutely nothing. She is my teacher. What I can't learn from her, can't be learned anywhere."

And with this, don Temo sighed and touched the Plexiglas covering his rug, running a dye-stained hand through his gray hair. Someone from the group of poets asked for the price of a long hallway runner in rust tones and he excused himself, gripping my hands with both of his and wishing me well.

Three months later I was in Ixcotel, the pungent themes of wonderment and magic overpowered with the realities of washing latrines and jockeying for space in the shower.

Soraya lifted a handful of magenta yarn from the jute bag at her feet, and said "today we make the sun rise." I watched her in the semi-circle of women crocheting bags, their hands gently moving in their laps, their heads bowed. Soraya didn't bow her head. She held her hands out in front of her chest as she worked, and kept her head straight, shoulders back. She was teaching the women how to add a new color to the purses that they would barter off through the social worker for enough yarn to crochet the next. To the whispering beiges and grays the women worked with steady hooks, Soraya insisted on adding a laughing magenta. Today they would add careful curves of triple shell stitches to their neutral bags—a sunburst dawning over somber countryside. "You will see how it changes with the sunrise." Soraya spoke in even, insistent tones, tinged by a Zapotec accent that turned her ordinary words to song.

I sat close to listen to Soraya speak. She kept her hair in a thick, unadorned braid and wore t-shirts and jeans. She was about 30 years old and had the poise of a priestess. But it was that voice that drew me in. Reports on the stale tortillas at lunch, or the splintered bench she sat on sounded exotic, dripping like cool Spanish moss over her native Zapotec, fricative and tonal. Early morning crickets and thrushes emerged from her throat.

From the first day, I noted that Soraya didn't form with the rest of us for roll call, but waited until we were in our places, and then walked quietly to hers. She did not look down as she walked, much like the native women who balance baskets of papayas on their head. She wholly trusted her step—seemed she had no voice inside screaming "you are trapped." Or maybe she didn't listen. The accent of this sure grace was as captivating as her speech.

Soraya showed me how to clean the latrine. She must have sensed my awkwardness. New women were assigned a week of latrine duty, and the obligatory three months of sweeping, the "*talacha.*" The boss lady said that they needed new brooms and pails, and offered me the chance to pay for material so I wouldn't have to sweep or clean the toilets. But being 'me' already carried some weighty benefits. I hadn't seen the Washington Post arrive to interview any of the others yet, and nobody else ate organic lettuce brought fresh from a friend's farm. Claiming additional privilege not only felt wrong, but dangerous. I had been warned by the guards not to leave any item untended, to send my clothes home to wash and to sleep with my watch on. Unaccustomed to being so wary, I decided to be just wary enough, and then draw close where I could, on the assumption that it is easiest to dislike what we know least about. I made myself more knowable so I wouldn't be more dislikable. And anyway—I didn't need less to do in a place where monotony was the flavor of the day. So I swept with the women, chatting about the dismal condition of the brooms or the high number of potato chip bags we had to sweep up on days the *rancho*, the prison food, was particularly inedible. And plunged my hands into latrines three times a day.

The latrine had two toilets with a short wall between them no more than a foot and a half tall, where women kept a supply of bottle caps for ashtrays. The bathroom had a door, but no privacy between the seatless, flushless toilets. A roughly cut swatch of flowered cotton hung across the opening to the shower stall that was barely wide enough to turn around in. The sink for washing our hands was the same one we washed clothes in outside in the courtyard, the same one we brushed our teeth in, and where we washed dishes after lunch.

"If you can manage to find three buckets in the courtyard, fill them so you'll have enough water to do both stalls and the shower. Berta usually tucks one away under the stairway so she'll have one to put her feet up on. You need to be fast, or they will sneak in behind you and use your buckets to flush. Sometimes it feels as if you'll never finish on the days when they serve bad beans in the morning, or when a whole group of us aligns with the moon. You'll get quicker after a while."

Soraya's voice could almost make you *want* to clean the latrines.

Early on, I begged Tomas to give me the true picture of the judicial panorama facing us. He said that, barring negotiations or other arrangements that might crop up, we could prepare for at least six months inside.

Six months.

He spelled out the steps. He trusted the law and knew this would work. I wished I could have found that inspiring. The filing for unconstitutionality, the request to submit witnesses, the subpoenaing of witnesses on their side. I was trampled by the idea of the upcoming battles to fight; the days after tedious days trying to stay focused on the next steps, the next skirmishes. The pleas, the letters, the witnesses, representatives and supporters. I asked a friend to bring me colored folders to organize the pieces. A green folder for incoming correspondence when friends printed out emails from my account. Brown for outgoing correspondence which they were generous enough to type out and send. Blue for the case, for lawyer notes. Purple for press, for new contacts, for anything that might indicate hope.

Self-defense wasn't something I had ever had to refine. To keep directed in Ixcotel, I chose to discard some of the petty daily battles that inevitably cropped up in confinement with other women. I would not fight for my 5pm shower.

Most of us took daily showers, so sometimes the cistern was empty at 5pm, but if there was water, it was warmed by a day's worth of sun, if there was sun. We had to shower quickly as the next woman was always waiting. I found a shower niche at 5pm, and claimed it by appearing with my flip flops and towel, shampoo and soap in hand. The door to the bathroom was a few feet from the semi-circle of women crocheting bags (now with budding sunbursts), and I sat for a moment with them, waiting for the 4:55 shower to end. Soraya held her bag as if it were fine silk. She wasn't speaking now; the women had learned their triple shells and crocheted in silence, except for acknowledging my presence.

"Time for your dunk, blondie?"

"I hope there's water. Sounds as if it's still falling from the showerhead. Listen."

"Just in time for the 5:30 roll call. You'll be fresh as a head of lettuce."

As I waited outside, Susa brushed by and commented on my purple towel as she passed on her way into the bathroom.

"Fourteen beets gave their lives for your towel, Gringa. Not a vegetable lover I see."

They called her a *malita*—one of the "bad girls" who got their nickname because of their crack habit. The *malitas* were obvious, hunkering down in the corner of the bathroom with their precious *piedritas* on a square of foil, and a cut-off straw to suck in the smoke. While we peed, while we showered, while we toweled dry and dressed. The only time they knew they had to leave was during scrub-down time, when there wasn't enough room for them to squat alongside our three buckets of water. There seemed to be an unspoken rule that the guards stayed out of the bathroom. In my effort to cause fewest ripples, I got along with Susa and the *malitas*. They hadn't been too interested in messing with me. I gave them sandwiches and cookies from the cache my friends brought daily, ripping a little piece off first, so it wouldn't be whole and they wouldn't be able to sell it for crack money. They always looked truly hungry.

When the 4:55-er came out, I stepped inside, but Susa was already undressed with crack tube in hand, sitting on the toilet and claiming next-shower rights, attending to three urgencies at the same time. I shrugged and left. Yes, I will fight the system. Yes I will fight to communicate. No, not for a 5pm shower.

I walked out and Soraya jumped to her feet.

"You shouldn't let her."

She seemed to suspect what was going on inside.

"I don't need to shower now. I've had a long day. I think I will rest some and take my shower after roll call." I sat with the crocheting women.

"No, it's not right."

Soraya took three long strides into the bathroom. I could hear her. We all could.

"You knew it was her turn. Doesn't she give you sandwiches? And she calls you by your rightful name? Some thanks. You might go fill a bucket in case the water runs out for her. I think that's what you really wanted to do. Now, go." Soraya's voice was smooth and magnetic.

Susa didn't seem to mind that all eyes were on her when she came out moments later.

"Hey, Gringuita. You go ahead. I just remembered I have something important to do. Sorry about that."

As far as I could hear, apologizing hadn't been one of Soraya's instructions.

The women nodded.

"She knew she was wrong," Soraya said as she came out behind Susa. Brushing fallen pomegranate leaves from her space on the wooden bench, she took up her crocheting. I sheepishly thanked her and said we would talk later, hurrying in to take my shower before anything else happened. I didn't want someone else fighting battles for me that I didn't deem important enough to fight myself. Soraya mistook my acceptance for resignation. The line is blurred, but palpable. I felt no defeat letting Susa have the shower, but maybe that came from not being stepped on enough. Anyway, I wasn't sure that Soraya was waging that battle solely on my behalf. Her strong words hammered at indignity. In Ixcotel, if you didn't arrive with dignity well anchored, it was unlikely you would leave with any. Soraya had dignity to spare—and seemed to believe a seed could take root in the cracks that appear in broken concrete. Or in Susa.

"I am in here to teach a man a lesson." She related her story one afternoon as we sat alone, she waiting for her crocheting circle to form after lunch, me with my notebook in hand, ruffling the pages I didn't want to fill.

"He is a well-known politician in my town. My father sold him rugs for years. I think he takes them to your country and people buy them for ten times their price. He dresses in blue suits and fancy polka-dot ties. I was helping with his ledgers. He would bring me a daisy in the morning, or touch my hair as I was leaving."

"You're beautiful, Soraya."

"Hmm. I know that. Do you say that to your wife, too?"

"My wife is not beautiful."

"But she loves you."

"Maybe."

Soraya needed the money at the end of the week. And anyway, he was pathetic. He ran the town through votes he bought with gifts of bricks, sacks of cement and shovels for people to build new houses. She knew this about him, and that he picked his nose and kept a bottle of hard liquor behind the law books on his shelf.

One evening, after replacing the third volume of the Civil Code for the Free and Sovereign State of Oaxaca, he locked the door

and came to her, fermented breath and tie like a limp snake, half uncoiled.

"I can give you beautiful things." He placed one hand on his zipper, another on her shoulder.

"I can give you fine purses. A satin ribbon for your braid. Would you like that?"

"I would like you to remove your hand from my shoulder."

"Ohhhh, difficult. I like difficult. Come, let's talk on the couch."

"You don't want to talk."

Still with one hand massaging his crotch, he reached for her breast and she stood straight, locking eyes with him.

"I have no more interest in you than I do a pig." She spat out the last words in Zapotec, so he wouldn't know how sharply she had insulted him, how deeply she hated him.

He was a well-known man in town, and could ill-afford a scandal. He had narrowly escaped being run out of town last year, when a visitor to his home noticed that his living room had the same marbleized tiles as the ones the citizens had bought for their town hall that was still marred by ugly cracked linoleum. He offered the visitor a few tiles for his own bathroom, and the incident remained in the mouths of few until the fellow noticed he had received all his tiles with broken corners. Suddenly, the scandal erupted and only blew over when the town's feast day that year came around and, thanks to their *politico*, the fireworks display was so bright and plentiful, the next town over enjoyed them as well.

"What would you like? A horse? I can get you a horse. Soraya, make an old man happy."

"I'm leaving now. And you will not stop me, or your wife will not be the only one disappointed in you."

"You are nothing but a stupid indian. Can't you see? I can make life very sweet for you—or I can make you wish you had chosen the sweet option."

Soraya's hand was already on the doorknob.

"I may be an indian, but I know two things. I know you will open this door now, and I know that nothing you do will leave a mark in my life. I won't let you hurt me."

Soraya twisted her braid in the only moment of vacillation I had seen in her since arriving.

"One week later I am here. For fraud. He faked his ledgers and said I had been misrepresenting his funds to him. Nonsense, of course. If I had taken $16,000 pesos I would certainly not have put up with the ongoing stink of his daily abuse."

"What does it look like for you, Soraya? Is your case advancing?"

"My father hired as good a lawyer as we can afford. It's been five months, but I'll soon be out, God willing. I will teach that man a lesson. That an indian is not stupid, and that his system may offer him a way to get rid of me for a time, but truth is on my side. My system can hurt him forever."

"What do you mean?"

"I can endure this. But when the sun rises on the morning after my release, the town will know enough to doubt him, or me, or both. I can live with their doubt—those who know me are very, very sure of me. But a politician? *Amiga*, who is sure of a politician?"

Soraya did not smile, but her voice had the merest glint of satisfaction.

That weekend was Soraya's birthday. Don Temo came to bring sweet tamales in corn husk packages tinted pink like the first wash of dawn.

"I see you have met my mysterious sunrise."

Soraya got out a few weeks later. I imagine that in her town, they now doubt their politician. And Soraya quietly hums as she collects pecan shells for the wool her father will dye to represent the old earth underneath a shade tree where they sat on her first afternoon home.

CASE NOTES II

If I felt minuscule next to the hulking greed that had landed me in Ixcotel and the sly movements of men who neglected to ask me what my best interests were as they were busy carrying them out, I was very thankful to have found a giant in Tomas. He wasn't afraid of any of them. Besides being a perceptive and thoughtful lawyer, he was a chess player. He had spent a lifetime outwitting opponents, in court and out. He knew the law, he knew strategy and he knew people.

Tomas said that he generally steered clear of involvement with the press, preferring to plot a straight case according to the rule of law, in which he deeply believed. He saw an uncluttered but slow-ish path to win our case through an *amparo*, a feature of Mexican law that allowed for claims of unconstitutionality on specified grounds. Nonetheless, given the profile of the accuser in this case and his potential ability to influence from within the system, Tomas did not discourage the flurry of press contacts and other links that our stalwart network of friends was busy orchestrating.

A reporter called from NPR, and we talked on the phone for ten minutes. In the episode of "All Things Considered" that aired that week, my ten minute interview was condensed to that one dense kernel that skilled reporters know how to ferret out, and a tiny voice that seemed impossibly mine said:

"Mexico has a justice system that is easily manipulated. Our charges are not a misunderstanding of something we did, but rather a total fabrication."

The NPR journalist interviewed the rector of the university, who denied ever having tried to evict Russell, though his signature appears on the eviction papers associated with the civil case. While we were in jail, federal officials arrived at Russell's home, and if their intention had been to remove him we never found out, as men and women from the village drove them off with barking dogs and sticks. The municipal president of the village defended Russell in the NPR interview by saying "He is a good person. He always lends his car when somebody has to go to the hospital. We have a lot of love for him here."

In that interview, Russell indicated that he thought the actions of the university were immoral. "They have come and taken my innocent friends. That is reason enough for me to dislike them."

The papers reported that the rector of the university/chief of police said we should have asked for permission to live on the land, that we were trespassing and deserved to be arrested. Still I wondered, if that were the case—if just by being present on the land we were trespassing, why did they have to invent the elaborate story with witnesses and violence and that phantom truck? Why weren't we jailed, then, for just being there?

In this desolate context where nothing made sense, I looked for shoots of hope everywhere. I remembered the time I spent in lands where people wake up every day with desolate bones and walk desolate earth--and still pull a shoot of hope from the muddied ground beneath them. Oddly, this story, this "fabrication," this fiction about our having violently usurped the land at Casa Ames gave me some small hope: it was a proof that the university wasn't sure of their story and had to resort to subterfuge to get their way. They had the power to put us in here, but only with lies. Truth must ultimately be on our side. Those who know us were very, very sure of us. But a politician? Who was sure of a politician?

CONCHA

The rats came out at night or early morning. When we unrolled ourselves from the cocoons where we slept on the concrete floor of the *cacahuate,* to pick our way to the bathroom, we caught them creeping along the sprawling branches of our pomegranate tree. In the delicate pre-dawn silence, we heard them lapping dew from the cupped leaves. During the day they took cover in the walls— except for one day when a disoriented rat scuttled into the prison-tinged light of late afternoon that, under clouds, might seem nearly-night. A few screams and the ridged sole of Concha's left sneaker stilled him. With 220 pounds of "gotcha," she squashed the fat gray rat into the stained patio of our communal courtyard. Gray on gray, with guts.

Concha was with her harem of young friends, gathered in a semi-circle around the little booth made of wobbly boards where Maritza sold toilet paper, laundry soap, gum and chips in colorful foil bags. It was the only place with a ready electric socket, and Concha had a boom box. With surprising phonetic accuracy, the girls sang along in English to pop tunes on tape. Concha spotted the rat as it darted out from behind the three garbage cans in the corner by the army of colorful brooms.

"Hey-Hey! *Una rata!*"

Concha was gleeful. Her voice broke through the contemplation of the crocheting circle, the buzz of the gossip circle and the chatter of the women scrubbing at the laundry sinks. Some women scattered in alarm, others gathered, curious.

"*Dios mío!*"

"Call the guards!"

"Don't be ridiculous. What would the guards do?"

"Be careful! Don't hurt it! Step on its tail!"

"Yeah, remember what it feels like to be cornered. Give him a chance!"

I watched from a distance in my shady spot under the pomegranate where I wrote, moving my pen against the page as the other women moved their crochet hooks through variegated strands of shiny nylon. The women gathered their yarns and rushed to put on their sandals, dispersing.

"Oh, but don't even think you are going to escape this, my friend!"

Concha leapt at the intruder as the women gave her wide berth. General mayhem fluttered from joyous to repulsive depending on where you stood. Concha was on her stage.

"This'll teach you to invade my turf you sneaky bastard! We'll sleep better with one less rat around, eh ladies?"

I thought the guards would come, or Concha would swat it with a broom. But her reputation as the roughest, surliest, most volatile woman in Ixcotel weighted her response. Concha and her rat became captives of each other. When a rolling groan oozed up from the crowd, most women turned away. I wrote "The tough woman crushed a rat with her foot" and watched as Concha used the disfigured rat as a soccer ball, making athletic passes through the courtyard. With triumphant bellows of laughter, she kicked her prize until she thought enough women had seen, and then left the remains behind the garbage cans with the timing of a stage professional, just before the crowd lost interest.

"He's out with the morning garbage! What you staring at? Never saw a lady kill a rat before?"

She shrugged, plunking down into her white plastic chair, patting at her sneakers as a *pistolero* would blow curls of smoke from his gun. She ran her hands through her short cap of curly hair spit through with silver and adjusted her tight "No Fear" tee shirt around her thick middle.

The rhythm of the afternoon resumed. The crocheters returned to their bench, and rested their bags of yarn at their feet.

I was first aware of Concha because of her size. On roll call the first day, I noticed a Gulliver of a woman surrounded by Lilliputians in the lines of the long-timers. Someone whistled at her and as she turned around, I was stunned by her playful face. From the back she was as hefty as any of the male guards, and I imagined a glower to match her size. But Concha's face wasn't hostile. It was remarkable for its absence of lines and its full cherubic cheeks under eyes that seemed to just barely hold a wink at bay. Her mischievous face was childlike, her proportions otherwise Amazonian. Maybe this made her pose for power more urgent. If you stopped at her face, you might have thought her a soft touch.

"Get any lately, Concha?" Berta shouted from a few lines over.

"Every night, my friend! Every night!" There was symmetry in her timbre and her body. She laughed large and full, throwing her strong arms around the young woman in front of her and kissing the top of her head. Anybody's guess if Concha's grab was welcome, as the woman just giggled, eyes downcast. Deep and resonant with a capricious edge, Concha's voice was a fog horn warning of a hulking danger below the surface.

At 29, Concha had already served seven of her fourteen sentenced years for armed robbery at a large bank in Mexico City. Capitalizing on the effect that her bulk and swagger had on the women, she had an entourage of handmaids who ironed her jeans, made sure her space in the shower was reserved and washed her clothes every third day. Her boom box music circle was closed, though. Few approached without invitation.

The day after the rat kill, I was sitting in the space I tagged to write, at a picnic table just off the courtyard in a sheltered corner. Beside me was an altar with a statue of the *Virgen de Guadalupe*. Her blue plaster cloak was nicked but her piety intact. Behind her, a faded poster print of the *Virgen*, and to one side, a creased *Virgen* postcard taped to the peach colored wall at a short person's eye level. The three *Virgenes* were all draped in a royal blue mantle peppered with stars, each standing on the curved belly of her own crescent moon. A spiky golden halo radiated from her cloak. She was dark skinned with sad, downcast eyes that made her approachable. To the women who invoked her she was more popular than Jesus and stronger than God himself. She posed serene and silent in her niche, her omnipotence cleverly disguised by gently folded hands.

I sat by the quiet *Virgen,* claiming a space to write. The women came to share a word or a nod with the Lady, but otherwise that corner was far away from the rumble, the gossip and shouts— only three steps removed, but within the radius of solemnity required by the *Virgenes.* I looked up from my writing when a shadow drifted in front of me. Concha had her arms crossed in front of her chest that jutted out like a shelf. She did not look happy.

"Can I have a word with you?"

"Yeah, sure…" I wondered under what circumstances someone would say "no" to Concha.

"You look a little sad, today, *Gringa.*" I expected some version of anger, and got insight. She bit the inside of her cheek and cocked her head to one side. She hadn't introduced herself, and straddling the bench on the other side of the table she drummed a syncopated riff on the tabletop with stubby fingers, stopped, and looked me in the eyes.

"Well?"

"Not sad, thinking."

"You do a lot of that." Could have been a question or a command. I saw I couldn't second-guess her.

"Thinking, planning, dreaming, whatever you call it. I write it down, anyway."

"You write, like, stories and stuff? I bet you write poems." I wasn't sure if she was mocking me. She gave a quick look over her shoulder and settled in on the bench.

"I only write notes to keep my pen moving. I'm like the women who crochet purses. Except I'm not great with a hook."

"They'd teach you, but stick to your writing. It makes you different. Not that you aren't already different enough!" She gave me a wink as if she were clueing me into a secret.

"I'm Concha by the way. Everyone here calls you *Gringa*, but I hear the guards called you *Mari* in roll call."

"Yeah. I'm *María Elena*."

"*Vaya vaya*! Yeah, right! A blondie with a Mexican name! Take that bone to another dog—No, what's your name, really?" Concha was loosening up, getting a kick out of herself. She rocked on the bench.

"Okay, so it's not the name on my birth certificate, but my parents just happened to give me a name that translates into Spanish."

"Maria Elena. Maria Elena—we figure you must be a teacher, since you speak Spanish and write all the time. You gonna teach us English?"

Concha didn't wait to hear if I was a teacher. She just barreled on, leaning in a little closer.

"I'm gonna tell ya something, but you have to promise not to tell anyone."

She tried to look threatening with absurd effect—the sun pretending to be hot. I smiled.

"Go ahead—promise!"

"I promise."

"Promise what?"

She was enjoying this.

"I promise not to tell anyone what you are going to tell me."

"Forever!"

"Forever."

"Okay, *Gringa*—at least don't tell anyone I know! You asked for it." Even though I hadn't.

"I write, too," she whispered.

"You write! Great! Now I won't be the only one!"

"Shhhhh! I said nobody knows. And you won't see me doing it here." She made a locking sign over her lips.

A friend who had been in prison in the States gave me a tip in the first days of my confinement in Ixcotel: blend in and buddy up to the toughest, meanest women there. I had muddled success with trying to blend. I swept with the women, but I had to hide my bloody blisters, blisters that I hoped never had the time to turn to callouses. Blisters held on to some softness inside. I sat in the circles of women that formed in the courtyard, but left suddenly to receive visitors, visitors with boxes and bags, shawls and pistachios. I wasn't having the greatest success in blending, but Concha took care of the buddying up. If bullies had wings, I was under one.

"So—you write poetry, right?"

"No, I'm just rehashing what the lawyer told me this morning, nothing creative. See these folders? The blue one has notes, the green one has letters coming in, the brown one has letters going out, and the yellow one has blank paper for new letters. It's like a job."

"Don't worry blondie. Someday you'll write the good stuff again."

Her incongruous pep talk made as much sense as anything in Ixcotel. I grabbed at the lifeline she tossed, even though it left me with questions. *What is the good stuff? When is 'again?'*

When we were alone, Concha was open and inquisitive. If someone walked by, she would jump in with a smart retort, louder than necessary.

"And that alley was black as the inside of a mean wolf's mouth! But I got away, easy!"

She wasn't hiding our friendship from the other women—she greeted me openly, even calling me by name from across the courtyard. What she did hide was this serious side that didn't fit with the wall of arrogance and bluster she cloaked herself in; a side that was seeping out during our talks by the *Virgen*. In pieces, she related parts of her past in detail I suspect not everyone got.

"I was only twenty-two when they caught up with me. I had already pulled off seven armed robberies in Mexico City when it all came down."

She didn't start as the leader, but she ended up as one after her older brother moved to "Da Bronz" in New York. But that last time in the Banamex on Insurgentes Street, she and her little gang were careless. The take had been effortless and quick. Not like the first times when the young crew was jumpy. After years of practice, they were perfectly choreographed. So they got cocky and didn't go straight back to the stash house.

"Cops caught up with us at a taco stand just as I was putting some green *habanero* sauce on my tacos. The yellow plastic squeeze bottle was grimy with fingerprints. Funny the details you remember about your last moments of freedom. I had just one bite before they were on me as fast as a skinny dog on garbage. They couldn't wait to take my greasy fingerprints back at the precinct."

The police found the take and the stocking masks in the back of the getaway Ford. Too easy. She was in the Penitentiary in Puebla for her first year, where she callused and quickened.

"You wouldn't have lasted a day in that miserable dungeon, Mari."

Concha wagged her head at me and smirked. "In Puebla they were tough. The place was full of crazies, real criminals. My first day in, the boss lady shoved me up against the ringleader so she could watch as we went at it on the floor of the mess hall. The rest of the women threw black beans and the breakfast eggs at us. Puebla made the women mean... It made all of us mean. I passed boss lady's test, though. Last time she *or* the ringleader tried anything with me."

When she was sentenced to thirteen more years, she was sent back to Oaxaca where her family lived nine long hours away from the prison: one hour walking, two in the back of a pickup truck, and six on the second class bus along the serpentine highway that led up from the coast. They brought her pictures of the cousins and homemade *quesillo* four times a year, but tried to stay in contact by phone. Concha was a regular in the phone lines, where she waited like everyone else to call her family. Except when she saw someone heading to a phone that happened to be free. Then she would shout "Hey-Hey!! It's reserved you know!" and nobody came back at her. Concha's communication to her hometown took two calls. After the first call to the public phone in the provisions store in San Mateo de los Bajos, the store attendant would announce the call over a speaker system that was heard throughout the town.

"Call for the Miranda family from Ixcotel State Prison!"

By the time Concha made it back to the front of the line, someone from her family had run to the store to receive her second call. The women made it a practice to stay away from Concha after she hung up with her family. Her gloomy gaze advised a no-approach zone.

"Were you afraid when you raided the banks, Concha? I mean... Twenty-two is young!"

"I was only afraid when the police showed up that last time. I was too excited to be afraid when we pulled the jobs. It was an adventure. It's all an adventure. Isn't it?"

"Were you afraid in Puebla?"

"Nah. Not afraid. Mad. In Puebla, we were all just criminals in a cage to the guards. And they treated all of us like the worst of us. Not like here. After that fight we were both sent to solitary lockdown. No chow for a few days. Not like here, Mari. This place is a party."

"Yeah, a real party."

"No, Mari. It was different. Trust me. They would have eaten you alive there. You're a teacher. That pen and notebook? These files?"

She tossed my color-coded files aside and they scattered.

"They would have sunk their claws right into your soft parts and ripped... you... apart!"

We sat looking into each other's eyes for a time. She was remembering and I was imagining. She had inadvertently thrown me another lifeline, as I imagined something worse than where I sat at that moment.

"And you, Concha? How did you make it through?"

"Absolutely, positively NO soft parts."

Concha's new gang inside was her circle of "girls," outside of which she didn't seem to have friends or enemies. The women steered clear. Nobody approached as she sat with her girls yowling along to the music every day, except during the *talacha* when we were required to sweep the entire courtyard. Most of the long-timers who were exempt from sweeping rose and lifted their white plastic stacking chairs so the bits of potato chip and candy wrappers from their lap would be whisked away with the rest of the mementos of a day's languishing. They remembered what it was like to sweep around the daily activities. Concha wouldn't move. Sometimes she would put her feet up on another chair and let the women sweep underneath. Or she would empty a coke on the ground in the path of a broom with an "Oops!" and only half-swallow her smirk.

I swept against the wall at the visiting grate during my midday sweep. Men who were allowed roaming privileges congregated outside our courtyard and the women brought *taquitos* and tortilla soup to them from the kitchen. I swept up cigarette butts, bits of lettuce and bottle caps from between the feet of the women who ignored me as they held hands through the bars with the men outside in the walkway. It made me feel like I was accomplishing something to haul so much away, leaving that section clear for a few minutes after my sweep. Swish, a clearing. As soon as the brooms quiet, the garbage begins to accumulate again. Sweeping was part of life there.

Two fellow *talacheras* who were fed up with Concha's antics, thought they saw a way around her that didn't involve confrontation—for them.

"You go sweep in Concha's circle today, *Gringa*. She likes you, doesn't she? I mean, maybe not like *that*, but we see you guys talking..."

"Yeah—see if she rips up a gum wrapper just to throw you something, like she does for us. Bet not!"

I rolled my eyes. I wasn't up for a game, but I knew Concha would prove them wrong. She wouldn't allow a public exception, and

I thought it would be a chance to "blend" more as the women saw that she didn't treat me any differently. Counting on Concha's unflinching public lack of cooperation, I moved toward where she sat.

"Hey, Mari!" Concha was sucking on a purple popsicle and wiped her mouth on her sleeve. "You got some time this afternoon?"

"I'll check my schedule and see if I can fit you in, Concha!" I made sure she saw my smile, and I started sweeping around her feet.

Then she stood, moved her chair, and picked up a few peanut shells from the ground. The two women watching threw their brooms down with an "I quit" look on their face that would have been comical if anything in Ixcotel could be.

"I gotta go check on my girls. See you this afternoon." She stuck the peanut shells in the pocket of her jeans.

"Oooh, *Gringa*! Concha likes you! What's she want from you, eh?"

Concha was the victor again, leaving us with a question on our lips.

That afternoon Concha came by as I wrote under the vigilant gaze of the *Virgen*. She kept looking over her shoulder.

"Waiting for someone?"

"No, just wanted to make sure… No, never mind." She didn't sit opposite me on the bench this time. She sidled alongside me, close. She smelled like Ivory soap.

"Hey, you ever… mind if I ask…" She was tugging on the wiry curls at the back of her head.

"What's up?"

"Listen… Have you… Have you ever been, you know… in love?" She looked at me through wide eyes, with a curiosity that forced furrows into her unlined forehead.

She was serious. Speaking of love in Ixcotel was like eating cotton candy in church. It didn't mesh with the gray, the smell of the toilets, the petty fights. Still, her incongruity was compelling.

"Yes, Concha. I've been in love. Why?"

She looked at me with a question as huge as any I had ever seen brought before the *Virgen*.

"Well, it's just... I think... Are you in love, like, now?"

"Yes, I am."

"I thought so. Does the other person know?"

"Yes, he does."

"How does he know?"

She picked at the splinters of wood on the tabletop, but kept her gaze fixed and anxious.

"I told him."

"You said 'I love you'? Weren't you afraid that he wouldn't say it back?"

"Well... I guess I just figured... I guess I just knew it was right. Sometimes you just know." *How had I known?* A lump started in my throat.

"But *how* do you just know?"

"Oh, Concha... I'm not the authority on these things. I just know... I just *knew* my own life. I said 'I love you' because I felt it from my heart. At the time it didn't matter if he felt the same thing."

"Well, does he?"

"Does he what?"

"Does he feel the same thing?"

Everything I knew to be safe and sure burst apart, how could I know anything for sure anymore?

"Mari? You okay?"

Her voice was low. She touched my hand and I landed.

"Yeah, sure. I'm fine. Sorry. Just thinking again."

Concha's hand stayed on mine for a moment, and I turned my palm up and lightly held hers.

"But, you were saying… You've got a few questions about love?"

Don't we all?

Concha shifted in her seat, leaning closer, and withdrew her hand, tucking them both beneath her.

"Yeah. I was wondering if you… maybe if you could help me with this letter for… for a person I know. I'm trying hard but it's really important. I don't want to mess up. Will you read it for me, Teach?"

Concha the Tough approached the uncertainty of love with her characteristic bravery.

"Sure, I can read it."

I read her three-page letter, shot through with the ache and vulnerability of a woman in love.

"Concha, you put a lot of emotion in here…"

"Yeah, but do you think this person will understand? I never used the word "love" before and it's a little scary…"

A woman who had carried a gun in bank heists in one of the largest cities in the world was scared of a word. But not just any word, *the* word. The ocean of differences between us receded, and in the course of the next twenty minutes on that rickety bench by the altar, Concha helped me understand her feelings of love for the recipient of her letter. She stumbled a little, and infused the usual clichés of love with her own brand of tenderness.

"I don't know if I will lay my head on your shoulder or you will lay your head on mine. I'm the tallest so it's easier for me. Someday we will be together. Might as well be here."

Tough Concha cracked open, buttery soft inside, with a crunch.

I helped her edit her letter down to one page that told someone, somewhere that she loved, authentically and earnestly.

"That's it. Yeah."

Concha folded the letter carefully to fit in the back pocket of her jeans.

"I have to write it now myself. I'll give it to her tomorrow. I can't stand another day without telling her."

She waited for a response from me.

"It's a good letter, Concha. It's a brave letter—just like you."

"Yeah, but what if she doesn't feel the same thing?"

"You may never know if you don't try."

"But…"

"But nothing."

How good it feels to throw a lifeline.

She rose slowly. Her vulnerability settled heavily on her—a tigress with a cupid's dart stuck in her huge paw.

"So how *did* you make it through Puebla, Concha? I thought you didn't have any soft parts!"

She made a locking sign over her lips, then turned and stalked, squaring her shoulders, back into the jungle.

Concha wasn't sleeping as often in the *cacahuate,* to the delight of the women who had been assigned spaces on either side of her.

"It's good to have room again! She took up more than her share."

"She was going to tell the boss lady I stole her pillow."

"She's rolling around with some girl in the dormitories. Good luck, I say."

The women felt relieved, as if a stone were shaken from their shoe.

Concha brought up the letter only once.

"Thanks for the letter, Teach."

"How'd it go?"

"Not sure yet. But for now it's good to have someone to ask questions with."

Exactamente, mi Concha.

Blackbirds in the Pomegranate Tree

CASE NOTES III

Tomas was waiting for me at the bars by the men's courtyard. John hadn't yet arrived. Stricken with polio as a child, Tomas walked with a slight limp and often with the assistance of a cane. He was my age. He had a warm and serious face and a voice that seemed perfectly modulated to impart calm. He felt like a friend, like solid ground and two steps forward. I was always so relieved to see him— it meant some news, something to be done, decisions, decisions and always a report on the chess game: he was every bit the communicator he promised to be, punctual, timely and clear. I was eager from the start to trust Tomas, and had a pretty keen sense that he deserved that trust.

He hadn't sat down yet, indicating for me to sit first. As he was about to sit beside me on the rough benches to wait for John, a prisoner on this side of the bars stopped him, greeted him with a hug, and spread a flattened page from an old newspaper for Tomas to sit on. "This'll do until the throne comes in, Doctor!" Seems I wasn't the only one who believed that Tomas deserved respect, in whatever form it would come.

When John arrived, Tomas went through the fifteen points of the *amparo* he was writing to challenge the constitutionality of the charges brought against us. He explained each point and I took notes so that I could explain them in English to friends. It was intense legalese that addressed the real definition of our "crime." The *amparo* proposed that the witnesses provided by the university did not prove that we entered the land with furtive and violent intent to take it over, such intent necessary for the crime with which we were charged. We were still somewhat amused by the implausible image of us "violently unloading furniture" on that cited fateful day. John swung his arm in the air and pretended to brandish a floor lamp with appropriate fury, and all three of us giggled. Just a little.

Additionally, the very existence of the civil case seemed to undo the validity of the charges against us. In the original civil proceedings, the university attempted to obtain possession of the land that they say is rightfully theirs, so while the civil case remained undecided, the university could not claim to actually *have* possession of the land they were denouncing us for supposedly having usurped. With the civil case pending, this criminal case against us was muddied with a chicken and egg conundrum and held no real weight. So said the *amparo* with thirteen other similar points that I struggled hard to understand. I think I did understand them in the moment that Tomas presented them. When he was gone, nothing made much sense. But I trusted him and he trusted the law, and we both trusted that moving every ounce of additional pressure from outside couldn't hurt.

Friends were calling on alumnae of the university to call back bequests. One who agreed to support our cause said "what I am pulling back from the university now is worth one hundred parcels of land. They'll feel this."

My old tourism agency threatened to hold back their planes going to Mexico, and Senator Leahy threatened to withhold aid money destined for Mexico, until we were released.

Friends were calling in more press: BBC, Chicago Tribune, Miami Herald, LA Times. My brother's hometown paper in Massachusetts got the story wrong and indicated that he was in jail. My own hometown paper ran that picture of Bill and me on Panda, and I received notes from old high school friends. "Help is on the way," one said. I hoped so.

We had Tomas' trust in the *amparo*, and an enormous movement on the outside pushing the story forward (before the age of social media, they knew how to crowdsource "old style," via phone, radio, television and email). Their support felt like the movements of the solar system—great universal, gravitational forces we couldn't see kept everything in orbit. Tomas had another plot afoot, and so did Tony and the consular agent, though not all at the same time and in the same vein. Next step, negotiation.

SUSA

I thought Susa was a man when I first saw her. A plaid shirt hung large on her shapeless body. No feminine curve softened her face, her eyes and cheeks hollowed too deeply into the skull beneath her sallow skin. She wore her dull hair chopped short as if with a child's blunt scissors, and spoke in a voice mottled with weariness, deep like a man's, emotionless.

Each day, she squatted in a shaded corner of the courtyard, where she had the best view of visitors' feet as they passed the guard station. The yellow plastic bucket at her ankles held brown polish, black polish, white polish and shine, in compact, round tins kept as clean as she could keep them with a wipe of her grimy rag. She made no effort to hide the jagged shards of broken, discolored teeth that snaggled her occasional smile. At thirty-four, Susa's lifetime of abuse could be read in the chiseled strokes across her face and withered hands, in the wilt of her bony shoulders.

"Hey, *Gringuita*, it's Wednesday. Maybe Señor Jaime'll bring you turkey sandwiches."

She looked off toward the ground, her words held more commentary than curiosity. A turkey sandwich is great, but it isn't a stash of *piedritas*. She knew I would give her a sandwich, unwrapped, with a piece torn off the corner so she couldn't sell it. Nobody traded crack for food. She would have no choice but to eat it.

"He'll be here in the afternoon, Susa."

"Good. Hey! I filled in for your *talacha* yesterday, when you saw your lawyer."

Susa had been inside long enough to be exempt from the *talacha* that we newly-arrived worked at six and noon, six and nine. Four times a day, we chose from the army of ragged, colorful brooms to sweep our courtyard into two cracked, grease-stained plastic cans with no lids and no liners. The garbage cans were emptied twice a day of what we swept up, of cigarettes, styrofoam cups and banana peels, of what is left when the juice is sucked away. New brooms were added only when somebody bought their way out of the *talacha*. Some women would sneak aside these stiffer brooms at night, or minutes before the sweep. The old brooms, splayed by overuse, recalled too many things to too many women. The newest broom was bright blue. Getting the blue broom was as good as some days would get.

"You don't need to work my *talacha*, Susa. I can make them up with latrine duty."

"Well, it's just that… Some people wonder. If your lawyer really visits that much. Jealous, I guess."

"The guards wouldn't let me out for any other reason."

"Don't worry. Just so they don't think you're getting special treatment because you are a *Gringa*. I don't mind sweeping for you."

"I'll see if I can tell the lawyer not to call for me at noon."

Jim arrived that afternoon, and Susa gave us scant minutes alone before she appeared and interrupted me mid-sentence.

"Hello, Señor Jaime, nice day, sir, lovely day… and sorry for the interruption and all, but can I offer a clean and shine for the gentleman's loafers?"

Jim said, "Well, sure" as if it were a novel idea. Susa placed her brick on the ground, nudging it three or four times into a perfect alignment that only she could see. She covered it with a clean, bright green paisley rag. She opened a tin of brown and a tin of shine and with her wide thumbs pushed polish into the leather seams of Jim's dusty shoes. She massaged his shoe gently, intently, as if it were a prince's weary foot. Then with streaked rags and brushes worn with grooves from buffing, she polished Jim's old shoes as he and I spoke of newspaper articles and human rights commissions and we avoided counting days.

Jim was one of the friends and neighbors who signed on to a daily rotation to bring food, water and a hug of solidarity to Ixcotel prison. Some of them could picture themselves inside. It could happen to anyone. I just happened to be the one living on land in dispute. Every day, someone planned and packed a meal and water for me, and enough chips, pistachios, Hershey's kisses or cookies for me to distribute. They drove out to wherever Ixcotel was, and waited in a miserably long line of visitors to be searched and questioned. They couldn't wear black—only the guards wore black. They couldn't bring fruit—it could be fermented to make spirits. They couldn't bring makeup or mirrors or manicure scissors—okay, the scissors— but mirrors? They sat with us in the compound, our connection to the outside. They saw where we slept and who we ate with. They never asked to use our bathrooms. Jim brought turkey sandwiches with pickle relish, and a great hug.

"There you go, señor. Like new." And they were.

"Susa, you're the best. And I've been around."

Susa smiled and didn't come back with any of the lines that she could have neatly added after Jim's wink. He reached for the fifty-peso bill he had already set aside, and pressed it into her hand, wiped cleanish with the green rag.

"See you next week, Señor Jaime. Thanks."

She kissed the purple bill, and stuffed the pesos into the side pocket of the jeans that were designed for a woman with more curves than she had, tucking the rag in after it and patting it softly. The brick fit into a net bag over her shoulder, and she headed toward the bathrooms.

I tried to imagine Susa before the crack, when she worked in her dad's taco stand "El Gordito" in Mexico City. Susa told me of those taco days, when she learned how to handle a cleaver and hacked at *carnitas,* dreaming of one day having a car.

"I was prettier then. Much prettier…" And her baritone voice disappeared into memory like a fist-sized stone dropped down a deep well.

Susa with shiny hair spilling to her waist. A blush in her full cheeks from the hot and arduous work of plunking freshly roasted pork legs on the chopping block. A full set of beautiful teeth. Susa laughing at the boys.

"Make mine hot and spicy, Susa, real hot!"

Her dad slapped the counter and shot them a dark look to shut them up. I imagined Susa before the addiction that tore out chunks of her youth with its ragged incisors.

Susa was the hardest working of the crack addicts in Ixcotel. Her shoeshine business earned her enough for what she needed most times, except on the sneaker days, when she would poke around for extra ironing or laundry.

"Doesn't anyone wear real shoes anymore? You'd think the whole world's running somewhere! All these sneakers…"

Susa didn't ask for money. She was different from the other addicts who carried a "got anything?" question on their lips as greeting. She knew I never had pesos. It was a condition I saw to after my second day in. Rosario only needed twenty pesos so she could buy scarlet yarn to crochet a purse, sell it for fifty, and return my investment. She got out fifteen minutes after the loan and I had my first inexpensive lesson. Need is denser than honesty. So I made it clear I didn't have money. I didn't buy items in the store where others bought laundry detergent, toothpaste or cookies. The women saw that friends brought me what I needed, plus enough to pass around.

My conspicuous consumption was limited to phone cards. I waited in line to buy them and then in line to call. I couldn't be without one, making sure I always had a fifty-peso card in reserve. I kept my hand in my pocket to feel the rounded edges of the hard plastic—my worry bead, my amulet, my drug. I made calls for a break from doing nothing. Or to connect with a person outside, with a calm voice that emanated from a place I might recognize. I was back in the line every hour. Susa asked for my spent cards with two pesos, three, five pesos left: not enough for me to call to New York or Cancún, but enough for the women who called locally. She sold them for crack cash. The leftovers from my habit fed hers.

Susa was in for robbery. This time. She had been in before, caught dealing drugs. When she got out that first time, she returned to her father's taco stand to work.

"*¡Estúpida niña idiota!*" her father screamed, pounding the counter with his fist. He hadn't forgiven her. She still dreamed of that car. One appeared to her on a dark and deserted street and Susa drove it for two days until the police caught up with her. She told the story as if it had happened a long time ago. Maybe it did. She said once that she didn't know whether it hurt more to count the time in or the time left, so she decided not to count at all.

"Heck of a place to lose my last few teeth."

We talked about getting out—I told her how I felt close to happy when the blackbirds fluttered in our pomegranate. Susa said she hoped for the miracle, though she wouldn't ask the *Virgen* for special favors.

"I just stay out of trouble. That *Virgen* has her hands full with people asking favors. You see them by her altar every day? You think the Lady has time for so many of us?"

For the crack addicts, the *malitas*, the bathroom was their invisible zone. The guards didn't enter. When we had to shower or shit, we were never alone. Some addicts needed to light up every half hour. Inside that zone, the *malitas* squatting against one gray wall were as present and eventually imperceptible as the mold. Foil saved from candies or kitchen scraps, cleaned and folded in neat squares, was cookstove for their *piedritas*, their precious little stones. With a straw cut short they sucked in wisps of consolation. In the bathroom, the crackheads rarely spoke or returned a greeting, and only raised their voices if they needed to flush. Then they would pass the flush bucket into the shower stall through the pink flowered sheet hung as a curtain. "Fill!"—and the showerer stopped in mid-lather to fill the bucket. The useless toilet mechanisms were no longer salvageable by rubber bands and string. The bucket worked if full enough and dumped from high over the bowl.

"Fill, please!" Susa passed me a bucket as I took my 5pm shower. She left an unwrapped bar of lavender soap inside.

"Susa, your soap."

"No, *Gringuita*. It's for you. Soraya gave it to me when she went free yesterday. She left a bunch of stuff. I don't need the soap."

She could have sold it for crack money. I thanked her and ran water from the shower into her bucket. With the bucket near full and my head full of lather, the water ran out.

"Damn!" I passed her the bucket.

"It's enough to flush." She threw the water into the toilet and it gurgled. "Don't worry, *Gringuita*. I can get you water from outside. Hang on."

And I finished scrubbing my head hoping that Susa meant it.

I had been warned by the guards and by other inmates on my first day in, to watch my belongings. To watch whom I sat next to. To watch absolutely everything, as everyone was on the take. I wrote in my journal on that first day:

I must be clear and calm. I must be intelligent and perceptive. I must be flexible and clever. I must be kind, but not too kind. I must understand that I am among others who may feel the same as I… or not.

Shampoo ran into my eyes. I held a towel to my forehead as I waited for Susa to return.

I very soon learned that I was not the lone innocent woman. There were plenty of us. Women tricked, framed, used as mules. Even the *malitas* could have been innocent. Maybe their habits started inside, a crutch for dealing with the impossibility of walls.

It was getting cold and I wanted to dress. I wondered if Susa would return.

The *malitas* kept to themselves. Except for Susa. When she wasn't working or hunkering down with her *piedritas*, she stopped to talk with me when I was writing in my corner by the *Virgen's* altar. She told me stories of her teen-aged son who occasionally sent her candy, and her mother who, god willing, would visit next month. I attached no motive to her friendliness. Some things in Ixcotel happened because other things didn't. There wasn't a lot to do. Maybe boredom drove Susa to talk with me. Maybe curiosity.

She returned with two buckets.

"I took it from the spigot by the kitchen. It's from the tank where the sun hits—should be warm."

One day Susa slipped into the seat across from me, running a bony, polish-splotched hand through her cropped hair. She was jumpy.

"*Gringuita*, you believe in the *Virgen*?" She aimed her chin over her shoulder to the images of the *Virgen de Guadalupe* at the altar.

"I think she's pretty cool," I said. "Nice clothes." I smiled and put my pen down, curious to see where the interview was headed.

"Well, guess what? The miracle happened! I am going home. *Santísima Virgen Madre!*"

As much as the news itself, Susa's sudden spurt of *Virgen*-mania riveted my attention.

"Wow, Susa! You must be thrilled!"

"Yeah, I found out today. But they won't let me out unless my family picks me up. I should call my mother. She can bring my son. I can hardly believe it!"

I had not seen Susa so animated.

"And you thought the *Virgen* was too busy!" I said. We locked gazes. Her face, unaccustomed to elation, looked strained from the effort of smiling.

"My mother's prayers, not mine. She's close to the Lady. Calls her Lupita."

"Well, they must know what they're doing! You said you had a lot of time left. What happened?"

"See that man here last week for me? No? He's a lawyer. My uncle sent him. He paid the right people, if you know what I mean. Said I could get out early—do time working with street kids or something. I'm not too sure about the details."

Susa unlocked her gaze from mine and fixed on the *Virgen's* toes.

"One thing, *Gringuita.* I don't have enough change to call Mexico City. Lend me an extra card? My mom can repay you when she picks me up."

"Let me check. I don't have one on me. Why don't you come back in a while?"

I had no safer spot than my own pockets for my amulets. I ran my fingers over two unused phone cards in my pocket, stroking the hard plastic. Release. The miracle. I so wanted to believe. Lies had turned my idyllic life inside out and shattered my impenetrable innocence. My case had been twisted like a crazy Rubik's cube, and I was alert to manipulations. But inside Ixcotel we condensed to primary colors and essential elements. Release. Blue. The miracle. Sky. I saw in front of me a friend asking a favor.

When Susa returned in an hour, I handed her an unused fifty-peso card, and another the next day to call her sister in Tijuana. Their mother had bad legs and couldn't travel alone. For freedom! With a third card she made the final confirmations on the day before her departure.

"My uncle works for Telmex. My mother'll bring you a bunch of cards, and her famous homemade pumpkin candy."

Susa piled her yellow bucket, net bag and brick with her pillows and blankets in a corner of the dormitory. Nobody wanted to take up the shoeshine trade after her. Too many sneaker and sandal days.

At noon, I met with Tomas. Though no more than an hour passed, I missed the arrival of Susa's mother. As soon as I returned to the women's courtyard, Susa handed me a note.

"My mother went to get bus tickets. We'll leave later tonight. Read the note she wrote."

In wobbly hand, her mother gave misspelled thanks for my befriending Susa. For helping her only daughter. The one that lent such light to her life. It recognized that some became friends in prison with people they might not meet on the outside. She was thankful that Susa and I found friendship here. And if I could lend her fifty pesos cash for food for the trip home...

"Let's talk later, Susa. I need to make a phone call now." Didn't Susa say she had a sister?

I called my own sister. Just to call. She told me that Senator Leahy made a statement in the Congressional record about the case. I heard her voice but couldn't connect with the fabled record entered by a Senator from a state not even my own. I was distracted by Susa mother's note.

Getting out. Our Holy Grail. I tangled Susa's excitement for release with my own, with everybody's release. I didn't hear the rest of what my sister said about Senator Leahy. It didn't have a key to the gate attached to it anyway, and Susa could just about hear her own keys jangling.

"Here, Susa. I only have thirty pesos. Take it."

"Oh, thanks! We won't need the money if the tickets are cheap. My mother can get a senior discount on hers."

Afternoon roll call passed, dusk, the last sweep. I pulled the blanket over my head in my corner of the floor as the soap operas sniveled on the television in our dormitory. I didn't see Susa, but her pile heaped in the corner like an old dog as I closed my eyes.

At 6:00 a.m. the tower woke us as every day. "Six a.m.— *Talacha! Talacha!*" I picked a path in the gray light, over the still-sleeping bodies of those who had been in prison long enough to skip morning chores. Susa curled in a question mark under her green plaid blanket and my heart sank.

I asked Berta, who knows everything. She and I worked in tandem as I flung buckets of water across the concrete floor, and she scrubbed with the blue broom she put aside the night before.

"Why didn't Susa leave yesterday?"

"Leave?" She gave a gold-speckled laugh. "Ooooh, Mari. Susa's not leavin' for a long time!"

"But didn't her mother arrive to pick her up?"

"Her mother? Nah, she never visits. She did the first time around. Not this time."

"Her son? What about her son?"

"Son? She doesn't have any kids that I know of. Don't think she ever sat still long enough to birth any. Has she been telling you stories?"

"I dunno." I started for another bucket.

"Here. I'll throw the buckets. You take the blue broom."

I sat that day with my back to the *Virgen* and wrote in my notebook.

"The tangle of women grabs me by the nape of my neck and pulls me under to their world. I sputter, floundering until I learn to breathe water, as they do."

I watched Susa walk through the courtyard, from corner to shadowed corner, with her brick in the net bag, and a newly laundered red rag stuffed into her pocket, eyes cast down at shoe level. She leaned into the doorway near where I wrote, but I looked right past her to the walls shedding their skin.

I was angry with Susa, with myself, with the mother who didn't come and the *Virgen* who didn't come through. I cursed Susa for seeing my frailties more clearly than I. I cursed myself for allowing myself to be hurt by hers.

I had shooed from the house as a pest, the possibility that her elaborate scheme was a trick. I wanted to believe in her release, and in her. And in us.

Hope fuels a huge business in lottery tickets and geranium seeds in Mexico. Hope raises children, builds homes from sheets of tin and begins again and again over and over.

On Wednesday, Jim brought turkey sandwiches and asked for his shoeshine.

"Susa must be doing laundry, Jim."

When he left, I broke a corner off a turkey sandwich and pitched the bread to the blackbirds in the pomegranate tree. A ruffle of wings in unison followed the bread as it landed in the dirt.

I found Susa on the roof patio.

"Here. I saved you something."

Her eyes lifted from the pile of unfolded t-shirts for a moment to hold mine. Tiny black stones, anchored with resignation.

"Next time you need anything, you tell me."

"I will, Susa, I will."

Her eyes returned to her work. She patted neat creases into a green t-shirt.

CASE NOTES IV

You could tell when it was a weekend in Ixcotel. Most often families came on weekends, traveling from distant villages to get there. The courtyard filled with more covered baskets of food, and the white chairs that stacked against the wall were all in use, pulled tight in huddles around a mother, a daughter, a wife. Bertha once spent an entire Saturday afternoon sewing, defending two empty chairs she had placed on either side of her for visitors who never came. At the end of visiting hours, she restacked the chairs without a word, poignantly defining loneliness with these last steps before the night's sweep.

My Mexican visitors came on weekends, and most of the Americans who visited me were retired and able to come at any time. I could count by the weekends, too, because each weekend inside, there was a heightened possibility that something would come together to bring us closer to release.

The very first weekend was the end of our six days "holding." We thought we would be out. That very first weekend, I talked with the judge and moments later received notice of imprisonment. It felt like coming closer to the gold ring on the merry-go-round. It's within reach now, my fingers feel the smooth metal and my horse speeds up on its own, out of sync with the speed of the countryside. Gone. The second weekend, there was to be a negotiation with the university. It seemed simple: the university wanted Russell to drop the countersuit, we wanted freedom. Of course the issue of the original civil suit brought by the university against Russell still dangled out there--any negotiation would have to include an assurance for Russell to stay in his home, as in the original plan. I insisted that Tomas be present in any negotiations with the university, though in the crazy patchwork overlap between civil and criminal cases, it seemed the negotiations were to be between Russell (through his motley representation via the civil case lawyer, Tony and the consular agent) and the university's lawyers.

Tony never entered the prison to visit—he was much too busy with much too much on the outside. He never fully accepted that we had dropped the first lawyer and Tony continued to discuss alternatives with him. Not unusual, because the lawyer was still responsible for the civil case, but we wanted the civil to stay separate, as we put our trust and our freedom, our release hopes in Tomas.

I called Tony from time to time because of his busy-ness on our behalf. Without communication I was unsure that he was moving in the direction that we, the imprisoned, wished. He knew what he was doing and saw a panorama that we couldn't—or so was his theory. Tony would say "You should be doing your best writing in there," and "I slept on the ground a lot, too, it isn't so bad, is it? Like camping!" I forgave him the bad jokes and bad taste. Few could really know what it felt like to be innocent and forced to live in a prison, no choice no voice. Few knew what to say. What I didn't forgive him, though, was the motive behind his movements "on our behalf," which became all too clear when, in an attempt to assure me that he was doing everything possible (as I hear the snap of the rubber gloves), he said he was pushing hard for this negotiation, "including for getting you guys out." Far from being assuring, that phrase took my breath away, and I heard little else of what he said after that, his priorities cutting dark and sharp as an obsidian blade. I had thought we were the purpose of the negotiation, not a fortunate inclusion.

So after the second weekend, marked by the negotiation with the university's lawyers, the gold ring came around again, and again my horse (perhaps prodded from behind) changed step at the last minute and the ring flew out of reach. I heard on Monday through a visit from the consular agent that the negotiations had failed. Russell was asking for too much. He was asking for easements and a reassessment of property lines. He was asking for a long list of specific details about the property... and also for our release. Somehow, that didn't sound like the Russell I knew. Tomas later corroborated that Russell sat by, silent, as others spoke for him. Russell was a romantic. He didn't care about easements. He wanted the land he had loved and loved on to be cherished. Though he now viewed the university as "immoral" for having imprisoned his innocent friends, Russell at 91 was far from understanding or caring about easements. A draft of the resolution that I saw presented seventeen very specific points that made demands of the university, some old, some new. I saw no point that offered the university anything in return. Though our release was stated in paragraph one, and I agreed with many of the points included there – it seemed a strange way to negotiate. Simply stated, "our side" (as represented by Tony and Russell's lawyer) wanted what it wanted and more. And the university was just going to have to suck it.

In his utopian world Russell just wanted things to be simple. And "simple" to him now meant following Tony's lead. And this is the way Tony was going. Not back to the simple, but on to bigger confrontation.

NATALIA

Women drifted in and out of the courtyard all day. Colorful butterfly women flitting, shadow women, sad wisps of women like smoke. Natalia appeared only when she had to—for roll call, mealtime, to reserve a spot at the laundry sinks. She had perfected imperceptibility by melting into the gray area between never being around and always being around. Nobody missed her presence—or absence. "The Phantasm" they called her, and women looked right through her unless they were bored, or had a bad dream the night before and needed someone to growl at. Natalia looked right back through them.

Her blotchy carnival-pink lipstick was out of place on a face that looked as if she had been brusquely shaken awake, her eyes in a squint, craving the comfort of dark. Rumpled creases engraved much too much grief on her face in nineteen short years. Looking as if it had been hastily cut in penance, her short brown hair was often matted at the back. It looked like Natalia spent a lot of time napping. She wore an oversized black sweater donated by Padre Osvaldo's parish—same sweater every day—her fists pulled deep inside the arms, shoulders hunched.

She had come to stare at the typing schedule posted just beside Jesus. A curious mix of the secular and devotional outfitted this altar in my writing corner. The crackled wall was the color of mamey with cream, writ with a history of change: nails, tape, tacks, holes, pictures added, then taken away. The wall held the three depictions of the *Virgen*, a picture of Jesus, and a worn photograph of a gray-templed priest who must have been important to somebody once. A short shelf covered by a rainbow shawl in double-shell crochet held plastic orchids and daffodils in a woven basket shrouded with months, years, lifetimes of dust. One natural and leafless rose, fat stem cut on diagonal, sat in an inch of water in a McCormick mayonnaise jar in front of the principle *Virgen,* yellow petals radiant against her cobalt robes. The last person who had set up her ironing board here left a can of spray starch and an unemptied bottlecap ashtray at the *Virgen's* feet.

When I didn't look up, Natalia slid in beside me. Without preamble, she thrust a folded page on the table in front of me.

"Maybe *you* can help with my letter." As if she had asked a thousand people before me.

The page she handed me had been torn into irregular pieces and coaxed back to whole with now-yellowed tape. The misaligned repair made me woozy. Natalia had written in simple block letters, words drawn and erased several times and smudged to a murky gray haze. Even through the interference, the startling account of a life ignited the page; a life painted in smoke tones, torn ragged and repaired as best she could. Fire, a railroad car, rats, songs, flowers— and a child.

"Will you help me?" She didn't look at me, and seemed to address the *Virgen*. But I knew she must have asked *her* already a hundred times or more. I was afraid to answer, uncertain how I could help.

"What's the fire you write about, Natalia?"

"Do you want me to tell you?"

"Do you want to?"

"Will you help me?"

We answered each other with questions. I suppressed my "How?"

I didn't know how I could help, and she probably didn't know either, but she needed some kind of answer. I gave her the wiggly-room one, and seemed enough for now.

"I'll try."

She took the letter back and folded it into quarters, the creases familiar to her, like those on a map to a favorite destination. The blurred words I had read sharpened and took frightening form as Natalia recounted her story of the fire, a railroad car, her rats, songs, flowers—and her child.

She came home from school that day with her third-year mathematics workbook heavy in her backpack. Kicking up dust on the dirt road home, she imagined how she would roll in the grass with Mina, her yellow dog, watching shadows change as the sun fattened like a ripe mango and came close enough to grab. Soft honeyed afternoon. She would sit down to dinner, perhaps chicken, and plop by the window to do homework. She would finish it quickly, to have time to brush her doll's long brown hair for one hundred strokes before bed. She saw herself smoothing the shiny locks over her doll's slim shoulders. Ninety-nine, one hundred.

Natalia never got home. A smoldering black scab had swallowed it. At the site of the reed house where her mother had rooted freckled geraniums in coffee cans, lay a stinking, charred skeleton. Her tire swing hung from a knobby branch of the plum tree. Checkered sheets twisted around the clothesline. Papi's rusty wheelbarrow reclined against the cinderblock shed, smugly intact. Natalia rubbed her fists into her eyes and crumbled onto the moistened earth. She would wait until Mami and Papi came home. Until Mina bounded into her lap. Until she awoke and the ruin of her home was as bright and whole as the swing and the tangled sheets and the gray shed. But the acrid smell of burned everything rose thick in a gray fog and stuck in her throat. The settling mess crackled and hissed, deceptively feigning survival. Her mind could form no questions—she could not stuff the enormity of this devastation into the miniature questions of "how?" or "why?"

Maybe Señor Gregorio would know what to do.

Natalia crossed the vacant field to the alfalfa farm where Señor Gregorio and his wife lived, looking back over her shoulder a few times to see if the scene had changed. A light breeze wiggled the swing. Would Señor Gregorio's home be gone, too? No, she could see it. Rushing her steps, she fell onto the grass, slashing green across the sleeve of her white school blouse.

"Uh-oh…" Her mother would be angry for the stain on the shirt, freshly ironed this morning. Pieces of meadow weeds clung to her hair.

From a few steps away, she saw Señor Gregorio and his wife pulling out their chairs at the dinner table. With chest heaving, she appeared in their doorway, wilted, her mouth a small "o."

"Oh, Natalia… There was a fire."

"Where is…"

"We're sorry. So, so sorry. We're trying to find your aunt in Veracruz."

"Yes, but where…"

"Do you want to stay here tonight?"

They didn't see that Natalia was a child in need of an answer. That at that moment she could not know what she wanted, beyond everything that had just vanished.

"Is Mina here?" Natalia formed her first question.

"Surely Mina ran away."

"Surely… and… Mami and Papi?"

"We're so sorry…"

Gregorio's wife set a bowl of warm chicken soup for Natalia, and with a motion of her chin showed her where to sit. Natalia did not want soup.

"Can I have some water, please?"

She gulped glass after glass, only stopping when she got the hiccups. They took her in that night, removing the lace doilies from the reclining chair she would use as a bed. They gave her a serape for cover, no pillow, and told her to be sure to go to the bathroom before she went to sleep.

"Gregorio, we can't keep that dim-witted girl—We can't take responsibility for her."

"Just tonight, dear. She needs to sleep somewhere."

"Let's make sure her aunt comes quickly. Or we can give Natalia bus fare for Veracruz."

"We've got to find her aunt first. We can't just send her off."

The next day Natalia returned to the rubble where her mother's washed sheets on the line were spotted with black ash. She bundled clothes in an old blanket from a heavy chest that had escaped the blaze. She tucked a water gourd into the backpack that still contained her mathematics book, and emptied the contents of the metal box that Mami kept inside the chest. A few coins clunked onto the floor and rolled in the ash, but she didn't bother to look for them. Already too much dust and memory clung to her skin. She took no inventory of what had disappeared and what was left behind.

"Mina Mina Mina Mina! *Mina Mina Mina Mina!*"

She followed the tracks toward town, and of every soul she met along the way she asked—"Have you seen my yellow dog?"

With small, blackened hands she balanced the pack of clothes on her head, as much to protect herself from the sun as to relieve the tedium of the load on her thin frame.

"Nah… but I have plenty of dogs at home—you can have a few of mine."

"I want Mina. Minaaa!"

Natalia traced the path of the rail tracks for half a day past town. When a train sped by she moved one step farther away than the stones could fly, and squatted, picking at blades of grass until it passed. She kept to the tracks because she couldn't think of what else, where else, how else to walk. Then, when she could not plod another step, she came upon an abandoned freight car behind a paper factory. It had been pulled off the tracks long ago, and settled now into the landscape, tall golden grasses growing in wayward tufts around its base. The old boxcar was rust-colored, though it may once have been the kind of vivid red car that transported the lions in a circus. The big sliding door was open a crack, enough for her to clamber up and squeeze through. She was wearing her uniform still, the white blouse under her plaid jumper wrinkled now, streaked by grass, ash and rust.

"What a good place for a dog to hide."

When her eyes adjusted to the inner cavern of the freight car, she saw it contained several barrels, a pile of old rags and a few bats hanging upside down from a wooden beam across the high ceiling. A scuffle in the corner made her heart jump and she imagined Mina, as a family of rats hid behind a stack of dented hubcaps. Giant black moths, camouflaged against the wall of the car, fluttered like ashen bits of memory as she moved through. She slumped into the rags. In the sudden cool of the dank corner, she emptied her bundle to pull her blanket around her, grimacing as the smell of that faraway day— was it yesterday?—leaped into her imagination. Pressing her palms over her eyelids, she summoned her mother's songs, hoping the rhymes would douse her anguish, as they had during a calamitous thunderstorm or after an unexpected tumble into the river. But Natalia's voice was wobbly and defeated, and the lullaby didn't work.

A little boat in a walnut shell

raised its little paper sail,

and left to the widest sea today

with golden honey to trade away.

She covered her head with the blanket and lay down, curled like a baby possum, sobbing into her fist.

Her aunt in Veracruz was old and couldn't walk. Natalia would not live with her. Not far from the river, here she could bathe and fetch water to wipe down the walls and floors. She was twelve, but she had learned to sweep, wipe, scrub and scare away vermin as she helped her mother, adding here, subtracting there, using this for that. Her mother had folded the cempazúchil seeds from last fall into the coarse paper that wrapped their tortillas. When her father's work shirt had more patches than shirt, it was torn into strips—one to fold into a wedge to prop up the short leg of the rickety kitchen table, several to tie into Natalia's curls at night, and a sleeve as a wind sock to predict oncoming storms. These memories of home wound into a tight knot in the center of Natalia's chest.

She scraped out a den for herself in that sullen and desolate space. The old boxcar became home for her, so aptly matching her mood, tarnished and tattered, appearing older than its years for being left forgotten and out of use. During four years, the knot inside her forced a grimace into her young face. It clenched her fists when they were empty, so that she had permanent half-moons etched onto her palms by her own fingernails.

She didn't see the grimace. Her only mirror was the river she slipped into each dawn, where she saw herself as patches of rippling color; a ghost-like, dream-like, diaphanous Natalia with rocks below the surface. Sometimes she curled the corners of her mouth at the blurred reflection, but any smile that would have wanted to respond rushed quickly downstream.

To ease the tension in her fists, she clung to marigolds and daisies, selling flowers to busy her hands. She passed out dollops of sunshine to people on the street in the next town farther up the tracks—for free the first time, investing from her mother's meager savings. She bought two bundles of zinnias and a basket of gardenias. Selling long stems by day and short corsage bouquets by night, she was able to buy enough for her household and to save toward a bicycle, though she wasn't sure she would know how to ride. The margins of her mathematics workbook were filigreed with simple sums, arrows and circles indicating what she had to spend on food and essentials, like blue corn.

"Hey you! I got some blue corn today. Eat it up eat it up eat eat… for you, yes… That's right. Matilde! Did you feed your babies? Be nice… There's enough for everyone… Now, time for a bedtime song."

In a barrel tipped onto its side, Natalia fed her rats, serenading them after dinner with snippets from her memorized scrapbook of songs—her mother's tunes now faded with age, she made up new ones.

"There is a castle in the clouds, a-shine and jeweled blue,

With diamond towers and sunlit harps, it's waiting just for you!"

She was careful to hang her own tortillas in a plastic bag high on a nail in the wall, trusting her rats but not tempting them as she was acquainted with the burden of hunger. There came a time, early on, when she let go of her hopes of finding Mina. Just as well—Mina might not understand her rats. She let spiders stay—respecting the hard work they put into their homes, invisible unless the sun streamed in through the broken board near the ceiling.

The pointleaf manzanita grows in the dry chaparral. Natalia gathered its leaves and fruit for a tea when her stomach wrenched. The manzanita with its wrinkly, deep red bark depends on heat from fires for long-term survival—its durable seed coat only scarifying to unlock dormancy after the highest temperatures of a blaze. Natalia was surviving by a latent instinct born of her own cataclysm, an instinct that helped her to know certain things.

She knew that her home in the boxcar should be kept secret. She knew starting time and quitting time at the nearby paper factory by the light of the morning and evening. Nothing so precise as a sailor who navigates by the position of the sun and stars, Natalia just knew, and was careful to slip in and out of her home like the rats, unheard, unseen. She knew which clients would be back for more flowers the next day, by the way they said *"Adios."* And she knew that she should not raise anyone's curiosity.

In town she made regular deliveries to cafes with her fists full of rainbows, saying little, always kissing the money received before placing it in a purse around her neck. She was as regular and expected as a good day's weariness. Notable more when she didn't show up than when she did. Upon a rare absence, a patron would sigh for the lack of her deep purple dahlias, not giving much thought to the young girl who sold them.

The years pushed Natalia's body into curves. It became harder for some—men mostly—not to notice her. Sometimes a man's hand would linger on her open palm when he dropped coins there, warmed from sitting in his pocket, such a private place. The slight touch aroused Natalia's curiosity. Other times boys on the street would shout "Come home with me and I'll buy all your flowers, doll!"

"I wonder where these boys live, Matilde. I bet they live in houses with chandeliers and a doorknocker in the shape of a woman's hand. I like their voices."

Natalia had learned about the sounds of sex from her parents, and the what-goes-where of sex from animals. She learned about the softs and hards the ups and downs the ins and outs and heartache of sex from Señor Florencio—who worked at the paper factory and who, on one still and sultry night left later than he was supposed to, catching a glimpse of Natalia as she slipped into her boxcar, wet from a dip into cool in the river, silvered by the moon.

Over the next few weeks he brought her flowers and new clothes. Flowers! These were not rusty-edged gardenias, bunched together with a rubber band, but roses! They glowed against the crackled wall of her boxcar. But when she held them to stop the tension in her fists after Florencio left, their thorns cut into her palms. Señor Florencio talked to her of things she had trouble understanding—but she loved to hear the soft hiss and sputter of his voice so close in her ears, like a symphony of morning birds.

He went to her in the evenings after work, and they would lie together on a new blanket with lavender circles and pink squares that he purchased in town. He asked her why she lived there—she told him. He asked her how she made a living—she told him. She hadn't trusted her story to anyone, but Señor Florencio loved her. He had said so. Only once, and only that first time, when it looked like she might not want the highest temperatures of a flash fire to break the dormancy of what she was holding inside.

"Let's."

"But…"

"C'mon."

"Wait, no…"

"Mmmmm… let's… I won't… yes, my love…"

"I don't know…"

"yes, my love… yes…"

So he loved her. Afterwards, comfortable in the fleck of warmth she found in his embrace, she asked him where he lived—he said "in town." She knew he worked at the paper factory, but when she asked him what he did there, he slapped her. Not hard, but the message was one she had already learned. No questions.

He apologized quickly, but looked over the top of her head when he spoke, not into her frightened eyes.

"You don't need to know so much and you don't need to ask."

"I won't ask any more. Please don't be mad!" Natalia didn't want him to go. She really didn't care about his life, just the wedge of it that crossed with hers. She liked that he was there with her, sometimes, and she could listen to his breath and feel his heavy arm across her shoulder in the almost-dark.

He always left her before night fully fell.

When she missed her cycle, she began to imagine how she would tell him. They would walk to the river, fingers linked, her thumb tracing the ridges of his knuckles. These hands would throw their child, giggling, into the air. When she was sure, she traced a small oval on the blanket where she pictured their baby would lie, and curved protectively around it. That afternoon, he didn't want to walk to the river. He unzipped his pants and hung them on the nail that should have held the tortillas. Brimming, bubbling she told him quickly "We are having a child." This time, the blow left a mark on her cheek, and she fell back onto the rumpled blanket, her mouth a small "o."

"Not this!"

"But…"

"But nothing! I've got my own kids to worry about!"

"You…"

"I've got to go."

"Will you be back?"

Her desperate question sputtered.

"What do you want from me, woman?"

He gave her questions when she needed answers. Natalia didn't know what she wanted, outside of what had suddenly appeared, like a curative dream on a night without stars.

Over the next several months, Señor Florencio checked in on her from time to time. She thought him a decent man. She didn't need more than he was giving. She wrapped her thin arms around herself, smooth and warm; the child embracing the child. She didn't look for the smile anymore in the rippled reflection in the river at dawn—she looked for her bulging belly. What Natalia remembered as happiness felt like quivers inside, like water dripping down her back from her long brown hair, like family found.

Her son was born on a Thursday, and Señor Florencio made sure that a midwife was there. He held the baby for a moment, and Natalia was moved to see tears in his eyes. He left quickly without saying a word.

The next day, police arrived at the abandoned boxcar in a black pickup truck carrying a club that one of them rapped against the side of her home to rouse her. She had not slept through the night, attentive to José as she introduced him to their life. But now in a haze of drowsiness, it seemed that something was dreadfully wrong with Señor Florencio—his name was the only sound she recognized in the broken dam of words that tumbled out of the policeman's mouth.

"What? What happened? Is he alright?"

"You'll have to come with us."

"Yes, yes! Of course! Let me get my son." José was lying in a basket with a red ribbon on the handle to scare away evil spirits.

"I'll take the baby."

"No, it's okay. I can hold him."

"I'll take the baby!"

And she clambered into the pickup truck where there was another policeman who held the baby who didn't bawl and didn't squirm and was every inch the gentleman she knew he would be— they had discussed manners on his first night home.

They drove to the precinct in silence, Natalia clenching her fists. When they arrived, Natalia followed the officers inside, where they opened a barred door and pushed her into a stone gray cell. A slam. The metal scrape of the key. Laughter. José was set, in his basket, on top of a manila file on a desktop, far, far beyond her reach.

He was so tiny, the question he wailed so vast it threatened to engulf them both. She closed her eyes tight against the onslaught of tears.

"Shhhh shhhhh, *pequeño*. There's got to be an answer."

Natalia clenched and unclenched her fists under the table.

"Natalia, that's an incredible story."

"It's not a story, it's true. It's here in the letter."

She unfolded the page again.

"Why is the page ripped?"

"It's not, it's back together."

"Did you tear it?"

"It tore."

Spanish verbs allow for this. No blame. One is absolved of being the causal agent in Spanish. I didn't drop it. It dropped. I didn't break it. It broke. She didn't tear it. It tore. It mended.

"Will you rewrite it so people will pay attention?"

I wanted so much to ask 'how?' It would be easier to translate her letter into Nahuatl. *So that they'll pay attention?* I could not ask her a question that neither of us could answer.

"I will try, Natalia."

Natalia's fervor for helping herself, for effecting release, for regaining her son was not evident in her language. Her sparse words in a child's voice were delicate and cryptic, like the flutter of invisible mosquitoes. I would restate her letter, and hope for the best. The next day I talked to Socorro, the social worker, who said that Natalia was better off inside.

"Look, here she can eat shrimp soup for lunch and has a roof over her head. Out there she was a kid living on her own. Who would take care of her now?"

I only saw the shrimp soup once in thirty-three days. The women told me it was flavored with shells, and anyone lucky enough to get a morsel of real shrimp ate it quickly to avoid envy. Socorro didn't know Natalia well, or she wouldn't have imagined ever, that she needed someone to take care of her.

"But doesn't she have the right to a lawyer? She is only nineteen—three years already she's been here. She can't live here the rest of her life now, can she?"

"There are no charges against her any more. The baby's father had a wife. She couldn't have children of her own it seems, and he already had several with other women. He only wanted to make his wife happy, and once she had a baby in her arms, they both dropped charges. The lawyers don't know what to do with Natalia."

"Did they close the case?"

"Not officially, but it seems that it closed for lack of attention."

It closed.

Standing in front of the altar, Natalia scrawled answers on a scrap of lined paper, on a napkin, on a flattened toilet paper tube. Perfectly imperceptible, she was just another woman in front of the blue robes of the *Virgen*, like the many who stood there hoping an answer would appear through the grace of their star-cloaked symbol of hope. But Natalia always found answers. She scrawled them herself, and kept them in a giant plastic jar that once held lollipops. She called them her "answers to impossible questions," and grabbed a crinkled handful to stuff in her pocket each time she left her room—the room to herself a perk of her three years inside, and a heavy snore.

I saw her use the answers on two occasions—the first on the day Concha killed the rat. Natalia was sitting with me before the showdown.

"I brought my birth certificate so you can see."

"Thanks, Natalia."

"It's ripped. That's the way my aunt brought it to me. She came here once."

"It's okay, you can still read it."

"My son doesn't have one. Not the right one anyway. I messed up."

"Natalia—it's not your fault."

"Maybe."

"You can't be with José right now. But he's not alone. He is cared for."

"But he doesn't know the songs."

"What songs?"

"Ours." She began to hum and move her lips, though I couldn't make out what she was singing. She walked away with her head down, arms pulled high into the sleeves of her sweater.

Moments later Concha had her meeting with the rat. Natalia was in the dark corner by the altar dreaming up another answer for her jar. The shouting began and she peeked out. She saw Concha and the lifeless rat, threw her hands over her face and ran to her room.

After the commotion passed, Concha resumed her position around the transistor radio with her harem. Not more than thirty minutes had passed when Natalia appeared from her room, hunched in her misshapen black sweater, her expressions a dictionary of pain. She held the jar of answers under one arm, and strode purposefully to Concha's circle, the tse tse to the tiger.

Concha treated Natalia as a bothersome little sister in front of the others, but had once told me that she identified with Natalia. Concha was nineteen when she arrived, Natalia's age now. She said people called her dense, but that Natalia had more sense packed into her teenage head than Concha herself had even now.

"Here."

"Heeeey, Nati! What's up, my friend?"

"Take them."

"What? Your answers?"

"Take them, Concha."

"Why?"

"I saw you kill that rat."

"Oh, Nati, c'mon, I…"

"Take an answer."

Concha looked at the women around her, and then to Natalia and shrugged. The harem women stifled laughter as Concha reached inside the jar, swishing her hand about in the fluff of papers.

"Here."

"No, it's your answer."

"So, what's the question, kiddo?"

"Why did you have to kill him like that?"

Concha stared, paralyzed for a millisecond by uncommon remorse, then shook her head and looked off into a far corner of the courtyard.

"Read it."

Concha unwadded the crimp of paper and read to herself. Without meeting Natalia's searing gaze, she got up, handed her the answer, and walked quickly away. Without looking at it, Natalia tossed the paper back in her tangle of answers, swirled it around, and relidded the jar to return to her room.

The next day Concha looked for me.

"She talks to them, you know. In the early morning, she walks out here in the courtyard, and she makes this little humming sound, maybe it's a song. I dunno. She likes the rats. Honest, I didn't think she'd be around… She's never… I didn't see her."

Concha´s voice lowered as she continued.

"I asked her once about this rat thing. If she always loved them. I mean, it's a little weird, isn't it? She said she loved them because of a song."

"A song?"

"Songs her mother used to sing. She taught me the one about the rats. And don't even ask because I'm not going to sing it here— no way. But these rats in the song? They were firemen. With little rat fireman hats and everything. Nothing will stop them from doing their job—you know. Blast a cat in the face with a firehose… I don't remember it all."

"A rat song."

"Yeah, rats are some kind of heroes for her. Everybody's gotta have one, I guess. She said once, her first heroes died with that fire. I think she, maybe like puppies do, imprinted on those rats in the rail car."

"Concha—what did your answer say that day?"

"Oh, the answer… the answer to the impossible question."

"Yeah—I saw you give it back to her."

"Weird… She asked me why I killed the rat, you know. And the answer said, no kidding, it said 'Someday you'll understand.' I don't know if that's me or Natalia who'll understand someday. What'ya think, Teach?"

"I guess you'll know someday."

Natalia checked in to see how I was doing with the letter. She always had an idea about something more to add, another detail of her life remembered.

"You can tell them José's hair is brown, like mine."

"It's almost done."

"Did you see what happened to Concha the other day?"

"What?"

"She was backed into a corner."

"What   do   you   mean?"
"She wouldn't have killed that rat. Not if she were alone with him. It was those people watching. They expected her to."

"You think so?" I was taken by Natalia's understanding of the nuances of a situation that was so horrific to her.

"I like rats, you know. Some people think that's weird. But they don't know them. They look away. I know them. I have slept with them, eaten with them, watched them have babies. They are good mothers. People think they are scary—but they don't know."

I rewrote the letter with bullet points:

• *I was born on March 12, 1985 (see attached copy of birth certificate)*

With eight bullet points ending with

• *I appeal to any and all individuals or groups that may be concerned about justice and human rights, to support my cause for release.*

I didn't write about the answers to impossible questions in there. I wanted to. I wanted to document the resolve of this young woman who kept a reserve of hope defined in a plastic jar beside her mattress, in a room the size of the warden's shoe closet. *La Fantasma*, the ghost, the imperceptible Natalia.

I talked to Padre Oswaldo when he came next time to bring clothes. To Socorro. To my friends. To my lawyer. They all got copies of Natalia's letter, taking it willingly, shaking their heads for any of a number of reasons.

The second time I encountered the answers was a few days after I distributed the letter. Natalia appeared quietly in the corner where I was writing. No one else was around. Thin young woman with long sleeves that dripped off the ends of her arms. Today she pulled her fists out from inside her sweater, clenched tightly around bits of paper. I hoped she hadn't torn the letter again. She opened both fists, and let a flurry of folded papers fall onto the wooden table in front of me.

"Take one."

"What are they, Natalia?"

"Answers."

"And what's the question?"

"Whatever you want it to be."

My answer was written on the corner of a Palmolive soap wrapper.

"Yes" it said.

Some answers are simple.

"Keep it—I have lots of answers left."

Concha said that we were all ghost women in Ixcotel, live ghost women turned invisible before our time.

"But we can't walk through walls. If we could, the world out there would be full of ghost women. Maybe it is already. Who would know?"

CASE NOTES V

I wrote Russell to try to get past the influence of Tony. Though Russell and I didn't have the decades together that he had with Tony, we had a close friendship forged through three years of eating meals and singing old temperance songs around his table, sharing intimate stories, burying a beloved dog, re-reading old manuscripts and love letters, and through oxygen tanks, dog bites, eye exams, hearing aids, false teeth and falls. He trusted me to be there for him. I once plunged my arm up to my elbow into Russell's ancient toilet because he said his teeth had fallen in. I found nothing. Drying my arm I went back to report, and looked at him closely.

"Smile, Russell."

"Why should I smile?"

"Just smile, c'mon, please?"

And his teeth shone white and even in his big, forced smile, as I patted at my last drops of water from his toilet in the crook of my elbow.

I had never needed Russell, but trusted that he would be there for me now that I did.

Tony insisted that the situation was more complicated than we realized (which I had no trouble understanding, that theme having been repeated by many). It felt like time, though, to condense the whole mess to its basic elements. Why skip the easy stuff? It seemed obvious that the university had no use for us inside as we were never any real threat—we were bargaining chips. If Russell would, plain and simple, give up the countersuit orchestrated by Tony, and go back to the original agreement, perhaps the university would let us go. This very basic negotiation hadn't been tried and seemed worth a shot. Tomas agreed to talk with Russell about this very simple plan, with the help of our American friends for translation.

"Russell, I beg you to consider going back to a simplest plan of returning to your original contract: agreeing to the university's terms of dropping the civil countersuit IF you can stay at home and we can be released swiftly and innocent, with no record of criminal charges. Can we try this simple step together? I think we agree that the value of freedom cannot be pitted against property lines and titles. We must all have our lives back... I miss you, Russell, and I hear you are well-attended. I hope Winnie continues to be a warm and certain comfort at your breakfast table."

The letter was delivered by two good friends from the community where we lived, American women who Russell trusted. We consulted no one other than our lawyer, and the letter flew directly in the face of the plots of Tony and his posse. If such a simple plan worked, the land would again be out of their hands, back where it belonged in the Ames' legacy to the university. When the consular agent learned that our friends had visited Russell and even introduced him to Tomas, he flew in a lather to Ixcotel. This time he didn't even pretend to come under the guise of bringing assistance to a distressed American prisoner. This time he arrived in a storm cloud to sow doubt about Tomas to me, to request that Tomas show him all documents that we will be signing, and anything that will be presented to Russell. He seemed to feel personally affronted by our recent actions, and even repeated various times that he hoped the "US Government wouldn't end up with egg on its face." The Embassy in a bigger sense, outside of Oaxaca, was involved as far as it could go. Officials kept family members informed, and advised on some points of law, like extradition. They were reportedly in touch with the State Department and moving what they could, but these seemed like lesser planets compared to the muscle being flexed by friends and relatives. And now the consular agent seemed to want to limit our movements in our own defense.

After that first negotiation failed, the university appeared to be feeling some effects of that flexing. Endowments were being rescinded thanks to friends who contacted alumnae, and they were receiving bad press on radio and in print. An international university with a large American interest, this negative press evidently weighed heavily on them. Full page ads were taken out in the local Oaxaca papers by other Mexican universities not wanting to be confused with "the one that jailed the Americans."

For the third weekend, we were drawing closer to what we came to call "the dog and pony show." Just as we were jailed on the whisper of an official into the judge's ear, Tomas had arranged for another staged move. Building on the university's growing wish to avoid public scandal, he wished to convince them that we didn't have to be inside for them to get what they wanted. He wished to convince them that they could release us, and save face. They wouldn't reverse their original charge—they were not about to say they had made a mistake. So it was decided that someone would again whisper to the judge and an opening would be made to allow us a special opportunity to present evidence out of cycle: we were not due to have this opportunity to present witnesses for another six months. From the beginning we had wanted Russell to testify, to tell them why we were with him on the land that he had bequeathed to the university upon his death--the land that would be theirs if they would just hang on for a bit while he walked a few more steps across the stone patio. Now we were to have that chance.

CITLALI

Burgundy and blue. The satin-sheen rags woven through Citlali's black braids and tied in a knot across her back were the color of afternoon skies that would forecast a storm. Furrows radiated from the corners of her eyes where she squinted for thirty-some years in the fields. In a grimy white chair, against a graying background of crumbling lime-washed block wall, she now squinted against a harsh sun that cast curly shadows from the concertina wire overhead. Petite sandaled feet were barely visible under her skirt woven of coarse dark wool. The front of the red blouse that hung loosely on her slight frame was graced by a tree in rainbow hues, sprawling from shoulder to shoulder. *Arco Iris.* Slung to one side and wrapped in checkered cloth, a child who appeared too large to comfortably carry was chewing on a fistful of her mother's braid.

The women told me that Citlali had been in for two years, and that when she first entered, she didn't know that this dark place was a prison. She didn't speak Spanish, and there were no Chinantec-speaking women in at the time. Mexican law requires the presence of a translator in judicial proceedings, and likely there was a translator present who spoke Zapotec, or Mixe or another indigenous language. Or maybe not.

She, as all women who enter, did not choose to come into this place. But she also came not knowing why, not knowing where, six months pregnant and, like all women who enter, wanting out.

Berta remembered her arrival.

"Those first few nights she slept outside, on the floor by the guards' post. Like she thought someone would open the door any minute and let her go home. *Pobre muchachita.*"

"With the rats? On the ground?"

Bad as it was inside, the *cacahuate* was four steps up from where the rats scurried at night, and had a floor that smelled pine-solvent clean. Still, she preferred to sleep without a roof.

"Yeah, weird, eh? Who knows… The boss lady would go fetch her every night and bring her back telling her it would be okay, shhhhhh, go back to sleep… You know. She would push Citlali back onto her mat. That poor woman kept repeating her Indian words like a chant, but boss lady never got it."

I recognized that willful freedom. Through my own journeys into indigenous lands, I discovered worlds that cannot be interpreted through the same eyes and ears that we use to understand our own realities. The indigenous way pokes through the soles of your feet and along those slumbering synapses that for most of us, haven't yet been stirred. Insistent, resistant, resilient and beguiling as any miracle in nature, the indigenous way did not allow for capture. They've been proving it for over five hundred years. No surprise Citlali was willing herself free.

Here you can eat regular meals and have a dry space to sleep, Citlali. Sometimes there is water in the shower and there are always enough people around to chat if that's what you feel like doing. But here they don't speak your language, do they, Citlali? Your words disappear on the wind as wisps of smoke around their ears. In prison *and* trapped by your tongue, the fetters gouge deeper into your ankles.

Of course, she knew now that she was imprisoned. Over the years, other Chinantec women had come and gone, some who spoke Spanish. I tried to talk with her, hoping she had learned enough Spanish to start.

"Your baby, is it a girl or a boy?"

"Is girl."

"Sweet. And how old is she?"

"Olid?"

"How many months?"

"Monss?"

"Yes, when was she born?" and I pretended to be counting on my fingers.

"Ah..." and she made rhythmic sounds like counting... "One..." and here Citlali made a sign like a circle. I assumed that the child was a year old, and that seemed to fit with the stories others told.

"They say she didn't scream when her baby was born. Not a sound."

"What is her name?"

"Flower. She is Li in Chinanteca. Xochitl for you. Xochitl flower..." and she began to sing softly in Chinantec to her child, strapped now to her front.

That was about as far as we could chat with conventional language, with the few words of Spanish that Citlali had picked up. I sat next to her in the courtyard as she sucked out the middle of a marrow bone and finished her broth, wiping clean the plastic bowl she brought when they served the *rancho* at midday, and tucking it into her sewing bag. Xochitl breast-fed under the vivid tree on her mother's blouse.

I stayed. I was drawn to Citlali as a hummingbird to a hibiscus. She talked to me softly, in a fluid, organic language that didn't fit with the angles, the clamor and concrete that contained us. Listening to Citlali, a supple jungle cloak gathered. She continued, and I listened to her cadence and waited for something that sounded like a question or a pause, so I could react. No question came. I think she was talking about Xochitl, because she kept stroking the plump thigh that stuck out from under her blouse. Then when the child was asleep, she slung her to one side and reached for her embroidery. This was Citlali's other language.

She removed a dozen wreaths of thread that she had wound herself, and laid them carefully on her lap. I had seen her sitting alone and painstakingly picking apart a length of thread into separate strands, winding each into those small coils. She continued talking to me in song-like vowels, soft slurring guttural stops and metallic-toned consonant licks. In her sparkling language, she told me about the piece she was working on, drawing the back of her hand across the threads as she spoke, with the same affection she showed when caressing her daughter's leg.

Rows of emerald French-knot corn stalks. Always the corn. There was a field bordered on the north by cross-stitched opalescent wind, on the south by topaz earth, east by ruby fire and western sapphire water. It was more than a sampler; it was a myth, a history. Two oxen pulled a cart full of needlepoint fruit. She cradled her hand under the cart as if to rock it, as she continued talking. I saw the sun, a ring of tangerine triangles, the moon, silver concentric circles. Her name, Citlali, was a star of radiant lemon light herringboned on a bright red background. Her daughter, Xochitl, a flower of delicate petals quite obviously born of that star. That is what I saw as she spoke. These designs were not solely ornamental. Even without full understanding, I knew their rococo complexity was intentional. Throughout Mexico and Central America, women wear these geometric expressions on their chests, a symbolic reflection of their own spirit, and the spirit of their ancestors. Not like the t-shirts sold in dollar stores that pronounce "I'm with stupid." Citlali's designs, like those created by Chinantec women before her, were intricate stories, allegories, beliefs and cautions. Worn where a woman's soul lies, where a child feeds, where clear broth warms on a chilly afternoon and memory sits, a barbed knot barely concealed.

Other women in Ixcotel embroidered fluffy pink peonies on tortilla napkins, or green quetzal birds on pillowcases. They sold these for enough money to make more, to keep busy while they waited for whatever came next; to not think about good memories that hurt, memories that crept into the spaces during idle hours. Citlali was making a library. She didn't sell her work. Her mother brought her new material every month. Her pieces were neatly stacked in a basket at her feet. So many stories expressed in thread fine as corn silk, unfolded in lines and curves across her woven page on the neat squares of red, blue or white fabric. She worked deliberately, methodically, prolifically—managing to create whole new worlds in the space of another woman's pre-stamped pink peony. Citlali had an urgency to express herself, though few could know exactly what she was saying. Given the context of the colors and the design, I could imagine. I blinked. It was like opening my eyes underwater beside a coral reef. Colorful and alluring, her stories resided in a realm that I admired but couldn't quite touch.

I once showed Citlali the scribbles in my notebook. I talked at length about what I was writing ... the case mostly. I mentioned the different colored pens I used and how my handwriting changed from morning to evening after eight hours of writing. How sometimes the pen almost broke through the paper when I was writing, and other times it was faint, tired. She stared intently at the pages, perhaps waiting for me to pause or intone a question. She reached out when I finished, running her fingers softly over the letters engraved by my pen. She motioned as if she were holding words in the palm of her hand, then touched her lips, and again the page. She smiled. Not something she did often, and the smile reached me from across the reef.

They were always in a patch of light, moving across the courtyard with the sun until it set – an event we couldn't actually see, but perceived by a change in shadows. Xochitl often sat by her mother's sewing bag, or was bundled to Citlali's side as she worked. There was no place to go. The courtyard was no more ample than the poorest man's cornfield, and she could walk no further than the bathrooms in one corner, the guard station in another, the wash basins to her right or the dormitories behind her. No door led to anything promising. Yet surrounded by this dreary exterior landscape Citlali released soaring birds, vanilla vines and plentiful harvests onto her canvas. She was creating hope from the most hopeless place. With the same *horror vacui* of the ancient indigenous artists, she would fill her weave with so much story, that the fabric underneath her designs was not distinguishable.

She lifted her right arm in a curve as she pulled her needle through. Then pointing with her needle to a winged pyramid of multi-colored rhombuses on the cloth she was working on, she said the Chinantec word for "warrior" and pointed to herself now with a descending motion from out of the sky above her head. Or maybe it was the word for "mother"… or "fountain"… or "bread." I had no way of knowing. Sometimes it was wonderful to imagine, a welcome exercise in creativity in the bleak context of the prison. But often I was left wishing I could decipher her. I didn't want to be another in the line of those who had misunderstood her.

"She's a witch, you know."

Xochitl must leave the jail in a year. Child protective services let babies stay in the prison with their mothers until their second birthday. Then they place them in public or private shelters, like the one run by Spanish nuns where I used to work with Lucia's little girl, before Ixcotel. Several youngsters lived in the compound with us, playing as any child would on a school playground or clinging to their mothers' skirts. I couldn't imagine Citlali without that little head peeking out from on her back. Even at a year old, Xochitl seemed to enjoy most the time spent wrapped close to her mother, watching her world, such as it was, from the security of her mother's embrace. Would Xochitl learn to sew? How would she learn to conjure hope? I imagined her leaving, protected by that colorful wrap, together with her star, her mother, her creator of worlds.

One day, Citlali was holding in her lap an older, somewhat ragged work on deepest blue, that she had taken from the bottom of her basket. It had a rush of white-trumpet morning glories surrounded by knotted black seeds. I sat down beside her to admire the trance-like grace of her design, and she said this time, a word I had heard before. "Ololiuqui."

"No, not a witch. She was a curandera *back there in San Juan Usila."*

"Ololiuqui." Citlali was making slow circles over the face of her bouquet of morning glories with both hands, chanting as if in prayer. I heard only two words I recognized, both flowers. Ololiuqui and Xochitl.

I knew Ololiuqui from a seed harvester I ran across when I had my first Mexican garden. I was learning all I could about plants that would grow in the extreme climates of Mexico. Ololiuqui is a morning glory, *rivea corymbosa*, that rambles wild throughout Latin America over great expanses of inhospitable countryside. Beautiful and tenacious in a natural state, the white trumpets glisten silver against the fiercely green heart-shaped leaves that cling to tree trunks and fences and meander across boulders. Ololiuqui seeds, round and hard as pebbles, have been sacred to the indigenous for millennia, prized for their power to heal and generate vision.

"Yeah, they say she's here for drug trafficking."

I noticed suddenly that Xochitl was not on her mother's back. Citlali did not look up from her lap as she continued the circles and the chant. "Xochitl... Ololiuqui... Ololiuqui... Ololiuqui... Xochitl." And she counted thirty black seeds on a deep blue background, one by one running her left index finger over them. I wished I could understand the numbers... learn to count in Chinantec... but maybe she wasn't reciting numbers. Maybe they were names, or wishes.

"...Not drugs. It was the mushrooms, the ones that make you dream..."

Citlali chanted, her face solemn.

The social worker brought Xochitl in from the doctor's office, and Citlali disrupted her chant and hurriedly placed the Ololiuqui bouquet inside her sewing bag. With a desperate question in her eyes, she spoke to the woman in Spanish, saying "Xochitl? Good?" The social worker said that the doctor had given her something for her fever, but it still remained pretty high and she should sleep. Citlali looked at the social worker as she spoke, and nodded "*sí, sí... sí.*" She lifted her child close to her breast, and wrapped her, heading slowly into their little room as the wind blew leaves off the pomegranate tree into her hair.

"Li, Li, Li."

"Who can translate for this woman?" I asked the social worker.

"Oh, we can call somebody in from the city in an emergency. Or in the men's section there are almost assuredly some Chinantecos. But all the child needs is sleep. She'll be fine. It's alright. Nothing to worry about."

A wisp of wind about our ears.

It was October and the rainy season had ended abruptly weeks earlier, promising dry skies until April. Yet this wind was cold and oddly moist. Dark clouds puffed in and it became apparent that a wayward Pacific storm was rustling up from the south. The women rushed inside, hoping that the television would keep them entertained while they kept their heads dry.

The first few drops fell like gobs of spit onto the gray concrete. I spotted Citlali's bag and placed it just inside the entrance to the dormitories where she would see it next time she came out. I went to sit by the altar to write of an unusual rain in a place without hope at a time of no one's choosing. I could see out the doorway to watch the rain as it fell like angry rivets, accompanied by startling rips of thunder.

Citlali appeared moments later in the doorway of her building. She removed her sandals, lifted the circlet of *rivea corymbosa* that she had created from threads as fine as her baby's hair, and walked out into the coursing rain. A windblown leaf stuck to her forehead and she removed it but held it in her right hand. In the center of the prison courtyard, the slow, monotonous daily pulse of women's lives vanished, replaced by the roar of the storm. Citlali looked skyward. Holding the deep blue cloth straight out in front of her, the trumpet blossoms and black nugget seeds were poised to catch the drops. She was moving her lips.

"Ololiuqui... Xochitl..." was all I understood.

A Chinantec from the men's complex could translate the words. But who can translate what is inside a woman's soul?

The thick needlework inscribing the fabric of her blouse kept her from soaking to the skin as she squatted now on the concrete with her face turned skyward still, her eyes closed. Her fingers moved deftly over the thirty seeds, counting. Or naming her hopes, one by one and starting again.

With the tough seed coats now moistened by the unexpected cloudburst, there may be tender, hopeful shoots to embroider tomorrow, visions, dreams feathered against the deep blue, as Citlali continues her story, and Xochitl sleeps.

CASE NOTES VI

Just in case, Tomas wanted to file his *amparo* at the latest possible date, giving space for any negotiations to demonstrate their effect, any dog and pony shows, any continued pressure from the State Department, from friends and press (without throwing anyone off with the sudden appearance of his well-studied defense). Our chess player calculated every move. The *amparo*, if granted—and he was sure it would be—would not have us released until the end of November, four more weekends. At this point we had been inside for three weekends, going on four, and Day of the Dead was approaching. Four more weekends felt a lifetime away.

Tomas had been to Russell's house. He reported back that my cats were beautiful, sitting on the window sills, and our dog Nini seemed to jump when she heard my name. Whether it was true or not didn't matter. It was nice to hear, and nice of him to say it.

Tomas was the voice of sanity in a storm of raging ego. Tony was said to be meeting with *campesinos* from nearby towns to learn about how to organize a land takeover. Peasants had been reclaiming land in Mexico since the Revolution of 1910. Tony certainly knew the right people to ask—though it was anybody's guess just what he planned to do. It certainly didn't sound like Tony was ready to let that land go. Even if we were released and the land reverted to its rightful owner with the university, Tony was looking at alternatives.

Meanwhile, Tomas listened, took note, met with officials on both sides, spoke softly, moved his pawns and made no enemies.

Going into the fourth weekend, we knew that an "agreement" was reached in conversations between government officials from the US, lawyers and the university, whereby the rector of the university acknowledged we were not squatters and should not have been arrested. However, the case would still have to proceed through special hearings, as the judge was requesting additional evidence demonstrating the rector's new admission. That evidence was available from the beginning. Russell would simply have to testify.

While I went my first day without visitors as the community prepared for Day of the Dead, the noise in the compound was deafening, excitement building around the day. More shouts, more laughter, more drums, more music, more insistence, more delirium, more more more. And I craved less. I craved quiet, whispers, my corner to write... even that had been taken away, the table turned into an altar. Dealing with the un-moderated noise of Ixcotel was a tougher adjustment than peeing with an audience. We all got used to communal toilets. I never got used to the noise. Even in sleep there were snores and groans – a reminder that we were not alone. I struggled to stay on the positive side of that message.

FLOR

"Macario was the woodcutter for a small village. Though the father of eleven children, all underclothed and malnourished, he didn't want anything of riches, nor did he wish to trade his poor lodgings for any other house. All he had, from the tender age of twenty, was a dream. This dream was to one day eat— reveling in the peace of the forest's depths, far from the famished stares of his young children—an entire roasted turkey, all on his own."

(B. Traven, from Macario)

The music started in the background and Mick Jagger screamed.

"I can't get no! Satisfaction! Cause I try, and I try, and I try, and I try..."

The prisoners gathered around the stage and sang along.

"Canna genno! Satee fachon!"

Macario, on stage, was dressed in white work clothes, a straw sombrero and dusty sandals. He carried a foil-covered cardboard machete. The crowd whistled and hooted at the opening of the first scene as the music faded and Macario dragged himself home to stage left, where a hammock was slung alongside a false hearth with a black cauldron that steamed with dry ice. His wife, dressed in the embroidered cloth of indigenous women, was kneeling and shaping tortillas between her palms. She welcomed him with an invitation to

dinner. "Black beans, green chile, tortillas, salt and lemongrass tea."
Like the day before and the day before that, the slump of Macario's weary
shoulders seemed to say.

The Stones re-entered:

"You can't always get what you want no, no, baby."

Macario is not a funny play. But the Stones lyrics punctuated
the play's central theme with such incongruous accuracy on that
peasant-dressed stage, that the disconnect connected. I smiled even
though I was supposed to be anywhere else but here. We were all as
out of place as that soundtrack. And it all made perfect sense for the
moment.

A month ago, Flor asked me to help with the play. I thought
it would look good on my resume. *State Penitentiary in Ixcotel, Oaxaca,
2003—English teacher, relationship counselor, translator, scribe, stage editor,
costume designer.* I never expected to be standing here watching. A
month ago I expected to be out by now.

Flor wore peacock heels and stockings. Blue, green, bright
poppy pumps. I wondered where she kept her kaleidoscope of shoes.
I had my two pair of pants and three shirts, an assortment of
underwear and one towel, always damp, in a plastic bag on a shelf
space assigned to me, tumbled alongside the bags and boxes
belonging to forty other women. Though she seemed to be around
my age, Flor hung out with the older women in the kitchen, two
tables down from my writing table. They smoked, and broke crisp
tortillas into bits to dunk into their steaming morning coffee.

"Mari!"

Each time I heard my name, hope coursed through me. A
phone call or a visit from Tomas, both gifts well out of proportion to
any other phone calls or visits at any other times or places in my life.

I passed by Flor as I left, and she stopped me. A sexy, scarlet
"U" blurred onto the rim of her coffee cup.

"Gringa—you a teacher?"

"No, sorry. I'm not."

"You look like a teacher. Not sure what that means, because look at me! I taught Civics. Think I look like one?" And she bubbled up with a guttural, rubied laugh.

"Sure—I'd say you look like one."

"That'll get you a long way here, sweetie."

I moved a step closer to the door, anxious to see what the guards wanted.

"When you get back from your visit, we can talk, blondie. There's something I want you to read."

Always the letters or song lyrics. I was the official reader and translator. But Flor had another thing in mind.

When I returned after my phone call from a friend, she invited me to her room where she had a worn book with the text for *Macario*. I knew the short story. It was written by one of my favorite authors—B. Traven, a foreigner who portrayed Mexico as his own. Flor had been in Ixcotel long enough to earn herself a room in the lottery. This one was smaller than my closet at Russell's house—large enough for a piece of plywood where she could lie down if she curled up like a sleeping cat. Her shoes were a tumble of pointed toes and worn straps. One pair of yellow pumps had duct tape around the heel. There was a single bare bulb in a ceiling that she had decorated with fluorescent stars pressed on in the shape of a heart. Pictures of her with friends and family were taped to one spot of wall, and she had a mirror. You could only see your face in it from a position on the plywood bed, but from the side I noticed that it had been glued together after a ragged crack had split it down the middle. Fat tears of glue dribbled down the shiny surface. I didn't want to look into it. I thought that maybe some of the strength I tried to keep close in Ixcotel was possible because I hadn't looked myself in the eyes. I hadn't seen the heaviness of desperation, the anger, the boredom, the tiny tiny hope, the vast depth of incredulity. The only reflection I saw of myself was in the small soft drink refrigerator close to my writing corner. I think I saw my hair getting long. Still, I was intrigued as it was the first mirror I had seen, outside of the little hand mirrors Ana used when she plucked her eyebrows.

"You have a mirror!"

"Yeah, such as it is. I look past that crack. It got easier after a while, y'know? We look past a lot of imperfections here. I'm forty-four, I'm here, I'm cracked down the center. Can't get away from the truth of a mirror. Hey—if you ever need to fix your hair or anything—I've got rollers. I have lipstick, too. I know they don't let the new women bring it in. And look! I have "Ciara"—you can wear it for the Day of the Dead party if you want. Only trouble is we'll all smell the same!"

"Thanks, Flor." I didn't tell her then that I figured I wouldn't be around for Day of the Dead. It was a whole month away. She had been in for four years. That next month stretched ahead of me like uncountable centuries, but to her, it was barely enough time to pull together her wild troupe of amateur actors. I didn't want to break the intimacy of the moment by admitting that we measured time by different ticks.

Flor had a small *Virgen de Guadalupe* tattooed on her back over her right shoulder. Said it was to keep people from stabbing her in the back. At least the faithful. She had a full Jayne Mansfield figure and her short skirts were probably tighter now than they were when she got in four years ago. Not much chance for exercise outside of walking—unless you were on the volleyball team, and Flor said it messed up her nails. The walk was enough for Flor. Seven minutes of winding concrete passageway, peppered with men who had privileges to be outside of their main courtyard. They sat on stumps or blankets and did their work—making soccer balls, wooden jigsaw puzzles, tiny bicycle reproductions out of electrical wire, or paintings of Mickey Mouse or Spanish galleons on burned-out light bulbs. They were rarely silent, especially when a woman walked by. In my case, I hoped the novelty of a fast-walking *gringa* would wear off soon enough. When Flor traveled that route, as she did daily to work with the theater group that met in the men's courtyard, even after four years the men raised their heads and whistled. She never minded. She hummed when she walked. Her dark hair, tinted with glowing ember highlights, was naturally curly and hung just below the length of her dangling silver earrings. Flor, by design, did not fade into any backgrounds.

We left her cramped quarters carrying the book, and approached my writing corner where I left a bottle of water when I ran off to the lawyer.

"You just leave this here?"

"I know. The guards told me to be careful. But I get water every day from my friends. If someone needs it enough to take it—they can have it."

"That'll get you a long way in here, toots."

I slid along the ragged bench leaving room for Flor, but she ran her hand across the wood and decided to stand.

"I have a cushion at my table. Gotta be careful with my nylons."

I moved closer and we looked through the well-read copy of B. Traven's *Macario* that Flor had obtained from the Prison Director. She said the Director was a poet. When she saw the crinkle of doubt on my face, she shrugged and repeated "He's a poet" with a strong nod that suggested I had better go along. Doing *Macario* for Day of the Dead was her idea. Part of it takes place on the feast day, and the protagonist, *muy mexicano*, blurs the line between hunger and satiety, good and evil, death and life. Great magic realism.

"Inventing another reality is a pastime these guys are good at. This oughta be a good story. You can help me convert it into a play, can't you?"

Bypassing this reality for a magical one wasn't a bad idea. "Sure, Flor. Can we get photocopies of the pages so that we could mark them up?"

"I'm sure the Director can help us with that," she said with a wink and raised just one eyebrow.

"Do we have costumes and scenery?" I asked.

"We have some stuff from our last play for Independence Day. We did *Los de Abajo*. Peasanty stuff that was donated by the church. If we need anything else, I'll see what we can get from the Director."

"Do you have audio equipment? And a sound system, microphones and all that?"

"Just a tape deck and some speakers. The Director usually gives us the background music. And everyone's voice carries well without microphones. They love this stuff. Nobody really listens anyway. We just have fun."

"Who is this Director, Flor?"

"That old poet up in the tower who signs your paycheck." She threw her head back and her long earrings tinkled with glints of silver in her cascade of curls. Her next words came through the snort of a laugh.

"And he's got a hand into everything here, kid. Literally." She ever-so-slightly hiked up the corner of her silky floral skirt and circled her hips, but stopped short with a wince and massaged the back of her neck.

"I shot a guy." Now she motioned for me to move aside so she could sit beside me. She walked slowly, her hand still resting on her neck, two tables away to pick up her cushion, and returned to throw it beside me, snuggling in and gently grabbing my forearm.

"I'm telling you this because you look like someone I can trust. If we're going to work together, I want you to know."

"It's fine—whatever you want to tell me." Their stories fell out. I didn't feel comfortable asking, following the unspoken rule: nobody had asked me my own story and I didn't ask back.

"I was a teacher in Sinaloa. Taught in the *secundaria*—Civics, like I said. My boyfriend, Román, was a drug runner for some big guys in Mexico City. I knew what he did. I didn't mind so much. I liked the idea of having guns around. Felt safer. You know, stuff goes on in the mountains. He taught me how to use them, just in case anyone came to our house unannounced. Mind if I smoke?"

"Yeah, Flor. No problem." In a prison full of women deprived of most things they love, breathing second-hand smoke was a negligible act of generosity. I was surprised that she asked. Flor lit a strong-smelling and curiously-named *Delicado*—the oval Mexican cigarettes favored by cowboys on the still-existing TV commercials. She played with her silver dangles and continued.

"We were out on a Sunday drive in the mountains, just having fun. Had food for a picnic in the back seat, a few cokes, a bottle of rum, tamales. In the trails behind the town, an SUV with tinted windows followed us for a few kilometers. I think Román knew we were in trouble, but he just turned the radio up and kept singing. *'Sigo Siendo el Rey.'*"

Flor stopped and looked off beyond me, beyond the *Virgen*, beyond the guard towers. She blew *Delicado* smoke into her memory of that day.

"Román pulled over and dug two guns from under the seat and threw one to me. I shot a guy. It was reflex—I had just taken a bullet in the back of the head. I whirled and pulled the trigger… Never knew who he was, but he died, and I'm in for homicide."

"The bullet in your head… Is that why you winced?"

"Life changes faster than you can say "don't shoot." The only thing I wanted was a room full of kids to teach, a house full of kids to feed, and Román. I had the classroom. I was pregnant when I came in here. Lost the baby. I see Román about once a month. He's out already. His guy didn't die. He comes and brings me stuff, but he's got another woman and a kid now. Maybe even a couple of 'em. And I've got a brain tumor."

"A brain tumor?"

"Well, that's what the doc says. A complication from the bullet. I need an operation, because it lays me flat sometimes. I do this theater stuff to keep my mind off the pain. The Director says he'll see to the operation. He's waiting for the state to approve it. Or waiting for another hot one to come along so he doesn't miss me while I'm gone. We all learn how best to get along in here, hon." She snorted again—no laughter this time.

Flor and I worked together on the play, focusing on the scenes that would work best on their stage. Macario in his home, Macario in the woods with the turkey, Macario in his new life as a rich man after a pact with the Devil. Flor had decided she would play the part of Death.

"This Death, she's a trickster, but let's see who tricks who!" She spoke already in the deep, forbidding voice that she would use on stage as Death. She grabbed the base of her skull and pretended to pull it from her shoulders, holding it high and saying "Alas, poor Flor, I knew her!"

I couldn't go to the rehearsals because I wasn't an official member of the group. I hadn't been there long enough to be considered, and I didn't want to know how long that took. After rehearsals, Flor came back to give me a report.

"Oooh! You shoulda seen him! Rigo, the guy who's playing Macario? He wants to change the scene in the woods with the turkey. He says the Devil takes up too much of the scene."

"Devils do that," I said. "What does Rigo want to change?"

"Well, if Rigo had his way, he'd have that Devil sprinkling salt on Macario's turkey from a sparkling silver shaker. "More, Sir?"" Flor put on the posh accent of a subservient devil.

"He figured if Macario's turkey dream came true, it might as well be a dream with all the fixings. In the end he agreed that the Devil could win, otherwise the story wouldn't get very far. But

Macario gets a few more lines before he gives in. I like what he did. They can rewrite stories and stir up some hope for their own, sorry predicament. Belief here is strong, strange as that sounds."

"I'll second that," I said, feigning belief in belief and making a mental note to consider it, later.

"The Director gave us music for the play that he picked out himself. I don't speak English, but he says it's perfect. You want to hear it?"

And before I had a chance to answer, she picked through the small plastic bag she kept her script in.

"Damn! I left the cassette in the rehearsal room. I'll bring it tomorrow."

Four weeks of rehearsals continued. For four weeks Flor and I forgot about the music. I had my notebooks, rewriting the formulas for parsing the scraps of information that filtered in from the lawyer, the outside world, family and friends. The recap of the play was a ten-minute diversion in each of my days—but even a ten-minute diversion is savored in a day whose choices were limited to where to sit and what time to call whom for five minutes.

Day of the Dead was a sensuous tangle in my memory. *Dia de Muertos* and its bright orange marigolds: *cempazúchil. Cempazúchil.* The name sounded like a golden birdcall. I could hear *cempazúchil,* smell its pungent herbal perfume, delight in the splashes of amber-honey-tangerine petals that adorned the altars on that day. *Borla,* the magenta cockscomb, a brooding intensity the color of votive candles in churches and the blush of excitement on young cheeks. I had been in Oaxaca on four of these days. On my first I was on a farm, where townspeople who dressed like death and the devil drank too much mezcal and fell to the ground after dizzying dances. The second I spent in the *Panteón de Santa Cruz* where Carmen had buried her husband. People brought beer, cigarettes, flowers and plates of turkey mole and hot chocolate for their departed families. Some played guitar and others sang or prayed in Zapotec. On the third I helped Piedad build a trail of *cempazúchil* petals from the road to her door, so the visiting souls wouldn't struggle to find the path to their earthly home. On the fourth I sat with Russell by the altar we built with pictures of Jean, as the wandering musicians came into his home and left him candies and a serenade in exchange for shots of mezcal. The preparations for Day of the Dead were the same here as outside—we had obtained the necessary altar items except for the alcohol, and the place smelled of wildflowers. But, like talking about love in a place that smells of latrines, *Dia de Muertos* didn't make sense for me in Ixcotel. I did not want to be here.

On the day of the big party, Concha asked if she could borrow a shirt to wear. Susa had a waiting list for shoeshines. I couldn't find a corner quiet enough. I wanted to crawl into Berta's little space under the bed and wish myself somewhere else. I went to the party only to see the play. I had to see Flor as trickster Death.

"When I'm drivin' in my car, and a man comes on the radio, he's telling me more and more about some useless information…"

I can't get no satisfaction.

The Director's choice of music was perfect, though he, John and I may have been the only ones to notice. I wondered, too, if he was listening from the crowd, or on closed-circuit television. His Flor, his flower, this Death dressed in black robes with a sash of marigold and *borla-* colored flowers.

She must have sat in front of her mirror to paint her beautiful face as a skull, white with great black circles around her eyes and lips. She had learned not to see the crack in the mirror, but today one black tear eased down her right cheek, as if traced from the pattern of glue that mocked her glamorous smile. On stage, her voice boomed across the crowd. Death cautioned Macario with a blend of mirth and reproach, and kept him thinking he had the upper hand, while the crowd see-sawed between rapt silence and belly-wrenching hilarity, even though the play, as written by Traven, was not at all funny.

Macario became a rich man, thinking he had the power of life and death in his hands. Death said (and Flor was ponderously, ominously Death) —"You do not... understand... the gift I gave you."

Macario died in the end, and Death... Death laughed or sobbed. Hard to tell. But the music swelled up and the crowd clapped and doña Flor bowed deep and low and raised the still-dead Macario by one limp arm so he could share in the accolades—but he refused to come to life. Flor dropped his arm and it plopped by his side. The crowd grew quickly silent.

Belief is strong. Macario's body was limp and still.

"Call the doctor! He's not moving!"

But Flor stayed in character.

"Macario!" she commanded. "Macario—you may not understand the gift I gave you—but you'll understand this kick I'm about to plant on your big, fat ass!"

Flor brought the house down, as Rigo leapt up and off the stage where his buddies raised him high on their shoulders.

"You can't always get what you want, but if you try sometimes you might find —

You get what you need!"

Flor said later that she identified more with Macario.

"I know what it's like to lose your dream. To get that old turkey to myself and gnaw down to the very bone, only to have it snatched away. And God knows, I know about making a pact with the Devil."

"So why'd you want to play the part of Death, Flor?"

"I've already made Macario's mistakes. It was time to feel how Death feels when she looks at us in our crazy lives, making a fucking mess of all we have."

"So how did Death feel?"

"Death wanted to give Macario the solid kick in the ass he deserved. I would have done it, you know. It would have felt so good."

One real tear streaked the white greasepaint as it fell down her cheek, a drop of glue binding death to her life.

CASE NOTES VII

When the judge decided there was insufficient evidence to release us, our hearts once again sank. Another weekend gone with no perceptible advance. Why wouldn't they just call Russell in? We were told by friends that the US Embassy instructed them to keep faith (they were doing everything possible), that Vicente Fox, the President of Mexico was to travel to the United States in the days that followed, and had meetings planned with state governors where this would undoubtedly be a topic of conversation. And if the State Department had not arranged it, friends with close-in contacts in Arizona and New Mexico were working on it as well. Or if the leaders preferred to talk about immigration or the war on drugs, we were assured our case would certainly be raised in higher level bilateral meetings to take place in Washington the following week. This week... the following week... and days dragged on. And fairy tales spun and the carrousel once again slowed... and the brass ring remained out of reach.

Ten days before the women in the *cacahuate* had given me the gift of a corner space to sleep. In the beginning, face-to-face with Berta, I was in the middle of the room and in direct sight line with the television. And every night at nine, when the women tuned into their soaps, I would cover my head with my blanket to block out the fluorescent light and the whining women on screen. When the woman in the corner spot in the back was freed, the others who slept in the *cacahuate* spoke with the boss lady to suggest that she assign me that space. They were watching out for me, again. "So she can sleep! Give her the dark corner!" they said. So for the last ten days I had the unearned but much-appreciated luxury of a corner space to sleep – nobody at my head, and nobody at my right side. And every night, as I turned to stare at the wall, I drew with my finger an imaginary tick mark and wondered if it would be my last. I couldn't feel the rough concrete under my finger. I had already formed callouses.

LUCÍA

Back in those six days of holding with scant communication, I looked for hope everywhere, only half believing there was anything to be hopeful about. On my second day in, the nuns arrived from the children's shelter where I had worked on weekends. In their pale blue habits and comfortable white shoes, they looked like salvation. Their incandescent glow illuminated the dismal walls of the prison and promised everything the threat of the prison did not. They were surely here to testify on my behalf, or because they knew someone important. They would explain that I read stories about crickets and whales to the children on Saturdays, that I helped bake cookies on Friendship Day and was a well-intentioned person, even if I wasn't Catholic anymore.

"*Santisima Maria Madre de Diós*! What are YOU doing here?"

They were surprised to see me. Thoughts of rescue scurried away like rats underfoot.

"Oh, sisters, you'll never believe... It was a terrible mistake..."

Sisters Inocencia and Tomasa had come to visit Noelia's mother. By chance they saw me sitting in the suite of gray offices where we stayed for the six interminable days and nights of due process. I was wearing the same clothes I had been picked up in, rumpled, and as ragged as the old sheet at the bottom of a laundry basket.

"No doubt! Tell us…" Sister Inocencia pushed at a wisp of graying hair that had loosened from under her pale blue habit.

"I was having dinner at home, and—" I stopped short. All of a sudden I couldn't catch my breath. Where could I start the story so it would make sense?

"There, now. It'll be alright." Their kind faces, programmed to console, were stricken with a concern that looked too much like pity to be comforting. They shook their heads and patted my hand.

"Remember there was a man who suffered much worse than this. And he wasn't guilty of anything."

"Neither am I, Sisters."

"Yes, yes. No, no, of course not. Oh, this is not right. What have you done?"

"Nothing, Sisters, nothing. Really. I'm innocent."

"Oh dear, oh dear. Surely there is somebody you can talk to."

They were disoriented. They held my hands and our blue eyes laced back and forth—theirs full of faith in things they couldn't see and mine afraid of the same.

"Dear, we only have a half hour, and we must see Noelia's mother."

"Yes, of course. I see. Please give Noelia and the kids a hug for me." Salvation was not to come through the Sisters.

They exchanged glances and shook their heads.

"We'll have the social worker look in on you. Soon. *Vaya con Diós.*" The Sisters hugged me as they padded off in their comfortable white shoes, and the rescue ship disappeared over the horizon.

"Noelia, you know you can't bring a lollipop into the library. You can stick it in the geranium pot on the sill, and pick it up on your way out."

Munchkin-sized and mischievous, she didn't earn her cuddles through her actions. She pulled Gloria's braid and stole from Eduardo the pretty book about the woman with rainbow fish in her hair. She ran out early to be first in line for snacks. Then she sneaked in with a lollipop under her tongue anyway. Noelia was impossible to discipline, and impossible to resist. She had learned that one infectious smile could cause a temporary memory lapse in adults. She would curl up in my lap and hold on. She might not have earned the cuddle, but she savored it.

We knew her mother was in jail. The sisters told me that Noelia went twice a month to the prison to visit her mother. At four years old, what could she understand of that space between them? I heard her say at the shelter once "My mother's house is bigger than this except there are no swings."

Shortly after I was committed to the main compound, a serious woman about my age sat down with me as I scribbled under the pomegranate tree. She carried a large ring of keys, obviously not a prisoner.

"You are Maria Elena."

It sounded like a command.

"Okay, yes, I am Maria Elena." Neither one of us made a motion to shake hands.

"The Sisters asked me to look in on you. Do you need help?"

"Depends on what you mean by 'help.'"

"As a social worker I can help women place their children, get medications, get a state appointed lawyer, or a translator and warm clothing if they need it."

Her lack of warmth was probably a product of these walls, and she had limits, too.

"Thanks… what did you say your name was?"

"Socorro. Socorro Paz Paredes."

"Emergency Peace Walls."

"*Perdón?*" Socorro did not speak English.

"No, sorry. Good name for a prison social worker, Socorro. I guess I don't need any of the help you can give. Unless one of those keys fits the exit gate and you'd be willing to lend it to me. But nice to know you are here for my *compañeras*. By the way, I guess the sisters told you I used to work at Santa Marta. Do you know little Noelia's mother?"

"Lucía. Yes, I know her. She has another small son from the conjugal visits here. Great idea to keep the desperation down, but then all these new kids crop up."

Socorro seemed to be blaming her heavy workload on prison sex.

"Lucía, she usually stays inside, in her room, but when she's out she sits with the women in that corner."

This corner, that corner. Socorro motioned to where the quiet women sat sewing. That corner where nothing else was going on, ever, except for quiet women sewing.

Our communal courtyard had six doorways: into the *cacahuate*, into the kitchen, into the altar for the *Virgen*, two entrances to dormitories in Sections A and B, and the bathroom/shower.

Visible in the courtyard were three washtubs where we wrung clothes, got water for the toilets, washed lunch dishes and brushed our teeth, the kiosk where Concha held court around her radio, the blackbird-filled pomegranate tree where I sat now with Socorro, the guards' tiny office, and the bars to the outside passageway through which I had met with reporters from the Washington Post and Associated Press. With no thought to the *feng shui* of our neighborhood, in plain sight and not far enough from the altar, three large plastic garbage cans posed in front of an array of mangled brooms. There was a set of broken steps up to the roof where women hung clothes to dry, and stacks of white plastic chairs that we pulled apart for ourselves and for our visitors, placing them now in a patch of shade, then in the sun for warmth.

This dreary background was tied together with concertina wire and the criss-cross of footsteps from one side to the other to the next up the steps down the steps into the kitchen to the guards to the garbage to the bathroom as clean as we could keep it from one side again to the other and over again. It wasn't a quiet space. The harsh sounds of inconformity ricocheted off the concrete and metal framework. Hacking, complaining, screeching, scratching, clanging. When there was laughter, and it was often, it usually came at the expense of something. Sometimes honesty, sometimes dignity, sometimes virtue.

"Lucia lives in Section B. She's got a six-month-old kid who was born inside. She gives me trouble. Lucia, not the child. It's her third time in. Noelia was born in jail, too. 'No' is not in Lucia's vocabulary with men. Seems she will do anything for them, including steal a car. That was her latest job."

I wasn't sure I wanted to know this much about Lucia, or about Socorro—but there it was.

"I'll introduce you next time I'm here."

"Thanks, Socorro. I'd appreciate that."

"Yeah. We'll see if you feel the same after you meet her."

Long before Socorro returned, I had figured it out. I listened during roll call. Four times a day the 110 women were together and I had the chance to hear the names, and see faces. The guards read "Lucia" from the list and a Noelia look-alike with a baby in her arms said "*Presente!*"

I didn't introduce myself to Lucia, yet. I waited for the next time Socorro breezed through dangling her keys and flipping through her notebook. She had come to tell Natalia that the women complained that she smelled rancid like old shoes, and she should change clothes more often. She caught Natalia in the coffee corner, where she was asking if anyone needed ironing done. Right there in front of everyone, Socorro cornered her.

"It's a disgrace, Natalia. You are old enough to know better."

Natalia, usually quiet, stared at the floor but defended herself.

"Miss Socorro, someone stole my red blouse. I told you that. I don't have anything else! If it weren't for Padre Osvaldo, I'd be naked."

Just then, Lucia walked through the kitchen to get milk for her baby. She heard "naked" and "Padre Osvaldo" and by the time Socorro scribbled in her notebook and put a serious period to her promise to get Natalia a shirt from somewhere, anywhere, even if it was a man's old workshirt, Lucia was in the corner where the quiet women sewed, spinning a tale about a lusty priest and a loose young woman who would do anything, anything for a new sweater.

She smiled a melting one, like Noelia, and quieted as Socorro approached.

"Lucia! What did we say about making up stories?"

"Ay, Socorro. Just having a little fun."

"Having fun at another person's expense gives you a short path to the director's office."

"Oooh! The Di-REC-tor!" Lucia put on a dramatic tone.

"Lucia!"

"And who did you bring me today, Señorita Paz Paredes?" Lucia smiled slyly.

"Lucia, this is Maria Elena. She works with the Sisters in Santa Marta."

"Worked, I think you mean. Right now it looks to me like she works with the Sisters of Ixcotel!"

I smiled, though I wasn't sure that Lucia intended to make me laugh. My hand offered in greeting was left in mid-air.

"So you know Noelia."

"I do. Everyone loves her. We call her the Princess of Lollipops. Nothing she likes better."

"You think I don't know that? I know that!"

We didn't start off well.

"I'm sorry, Lucia. I didn't mean… Any time you want to … want to talk about Noelia—I'd love to hear your stories."

"Oh, now you're going to test me to see what I know? Well I know plenty!" Her voice rose in menacing pitch.

Socorro stepped in. "Lucia! Calm down."

"I have to go now." And she tried to get by Socorro, who stopped her by grabbing her arm.

"I think you should apologize first to Maria Elena."

"I should do a lot of things." Socorro didn't hold onto her. Lucia turned and walked to her dormitory.

Later, I heard from some of the women that Lucia was whispering stories about me. That I was paying off the boss lady in food, though she wasn't telling them what favors I was getting in exchange.

"But it's not true. Is it?" the women asked.

"Of course it's not true. You guys get all my food!" And the group of us sitting in that corner laughed, just for the heck of it.

Lucia approached me as I was getting off the phone. Her son was screaming and she put one hand over his mouth as she talked.

"Hey. I'm sorry about the other day. I was just touchy."

"It's okay, Lucia."

"Do you have any phone cards that you can spare?"

A calculated apology. As interesting as it would be to see how she treated the people on her "good" list, her request came on the heels of my incident with Susa, and I wasn't giving phone cards to anyone.

"Sorry, Lucia. Nothing extra."

"No extras. No extras. Just to Susa, I guess. She give you crack? Or something else?"

"Sorry, Lucia." I had nothing to say.

"Here, hold him for a minute, would ya?" She thrust her child at me as he screamed, red in the face. She was searching inside a plastic bag.

"Okay, no phone cards, but how about ten pesos? I want to buy Noelia some candy for when she visits. Look, this is all I have."

And she took out two pesos fifty from her bag. Her son stopped fussing in my arms and focused on the shiny coins.

"No, Lucia. I don't have any cash on me." There was nothing more to say. I wouldn't be making it to her good side just now. At least her son had quieted.

"Fine. C'mon Sami. Let's go sit with some real friends." She grabbed her baby so hard his face became red and wrinkled and his mouth opened wide as another scream let loose across the courtyard.

The Princess of Lollipops floated in, well-behaved and holding onto Socorro's hand one Sunday. I wanted to run out and squeeze her into one of her signature mischievous smiles. I was by the *Virgen*, writing. But of course she hadn't come to see me. I saw that Lucia waited, in a chair in the corner where the quiet women sewed.

As Socorro arrived with Noelia by the hand.

And Noelia kissed her mother on the cheek.

And Socorro pulled up two more stacking chairs.

As Noelia sat with her hands in her lap.

And Socorro did most of the talking, referee style between the mom and her fidgety daughter.

As Noelia smiled.

And Lucia didn't.

And Socorro looked at her watch and instructed Noelia to kiss her mother good-bye, which she did, softly, on the cheek.

And Socorro stacked two plastic chairs back against the wall.

As Lucia walked away.

Noelia had only known her mother in the context of Ixcotel prison. Twice a month for four years. She had only known me, once a week for two, in the library of the children's shelter.

When Socorro brought little Noelia into my corner, her clever young eyes widened and she struggled to recognize me. Like seeing the Three Kings arrive in Summer. She knew something was right and something was wrong, but didn't know exactly what.

"Are you here to visit my mama, too?"

"Yes, Noelia." I wasn't sure how much she would understand.

She dropped Socorro's hand and ran to me and lifted her arms high. I picked her up easily and she held me around the neck and said "Read me a story!"

I'm not sure which of us felt more found at that moment.

I settled her on my lap, and gave her a lollipop from the stash my friends brought. A Tootsie Pop that lasts forever. To pass the time, they said. She held it for a moment, but let it drop to the floor to hug me again when Socorro said it was time to go.

"Let's go! The Sisters are waiting for us." Noelia scampered off my lap and grabbed at my hand to go with her.

"Maria Elena will stay here for now, Noelia." Socorro eased her away by the shoulders.

"No! She needs to tell us stories!" She cried into Socorro's skirt.

"Another time," I said.

"Another time," said Socorro.

For days after Noelia's visit, any time I got up from my seat in a white plastic chair—in the sun, in the shade—Lucia was there when I returned, staring at me with her arms folded across her chest and a dare in her expression that I chose not to engage. She stepped in front of me in the phone line, and I walked away. Anger rumbled so close to the surface for most of us—it was dangerous to scratch at it. I wasn't a fighter and I couldn't imagine how to make peace with Lucia, so I ignored her. She twice knocked my notebooks off the corner of the table where I was writing and once my salad was missing from the kitchen refrigerator. Nobody liked the food I ate. The organic lettuce my friends brought wasn't a temptation to others. I didn't know that it was Lucia who had taken my salad until a few days later when Efigia gave me the Tupperware full of wilted greens that she found in the sink after Lucia had washed Sami's bottles.

I could continue to ignore her. I had managed to stay in a bubble of non-aggression, and despite the mélange of angers we each carried around with us, I never felt tested to release my own with the women. The bonds of solidarity that united us repelled a good amount of our anger. Lucia was acting bitchy, certainly, but she was stuck here like the rest of us. I couldn't subtract that shared circumstance from the picture. Nothing that Lucia was doing around me had yet been too much to take. In the scale of annoyances at Ixcotel, stealing my chair was an almost comical one. But I was stumped at her real motive—and that bothered me more than seemed appropriate, perhaps because I was already over-sensitive to being blamed for things I hadn't done.

A visit from Socorro changed everything.

The following weekend she brought an envelope to Lucia where she sat in that corner with the quiet women. Lucia opened it and unfolded the page from inside, staring blankly for several seconds and sending Socorro away with no word and a wave. She looked angry, and glanced in my direction, then back at the page. She pushed her chair back violently and strode over to where I sat, waving the page in my face.

"You didn't get one of these, did you? Did you?"

"No, Lucia. I don't know what it is." The fluttering page seemed to contain a child's drawing.

"Nothing. Never mind. Socorro didn't bring you a letter?"

"No."

"Liar!" She turned and rushed into Dormitory B.

Over the next few days Lucia's mischief with me stopped completely. She was rarely around. When she did appear, she sat quietly, with Sami, and was never without that envelope. She would open it, take out the page, stare at it and then place it back inside. Minutes later she would unfold it again, as if checking to see if anything had changed. Whatever that note contained, it had captivated Lucia.

Then one day she pulled up a chair.

"You think Noelia is happy there?" She looked off into a corner.

I didn't know what she wanted to hear, and I didn't take time to weigh the options. I told her the truth.

"Yeah, Lucia. I think she's happy. She likes her playmates. The shelter is a fun place for the kids, and the Sisters love them."

"I used to think she and I had a lot in common—we were both in jail."

Lucía bit her lip and looked far past the blackbirds in the pomegranate.

"She didn't choose to be there, and I didn't choose to be here. Socorro said I did choose, but she doesn't know."

I didn't respond. It felt comfortable to let silence sit between us for a moment.

"We don't have so much in common, my girl and me. I could be more like her. She's happy with so little."

Looks like Noelia had coaxed Lucia toward her own redemption. She was trying to figure some things out, taking a lesson from her child.

"I saw you give her that lollipop."

I understood for the first time, that Lucia was watching that afternoon that Noelia sat on my lap.

"You wouldn't give me money to buy candy for her! And all along you had her favorite thing. That was a dirty trick."

"I'm sorry, Lucia. I wasn't thinking."

"Yeah, but anyway—I saw her drop it. That served you right, I thought. But her face! She didn't want it. She didn't want her lollipop. She wanted you. And your stories."

"That's all she's ever seen me do. That's all she ever wants from me."

"I've never read her a story. I don't know how to read."

Lucia looked at me, and I couldn't tell if the blush in her cheek was anger or something else.

"She never listened to my stories, Lucia. She remembers me with a book. That makes sense to her I guess."

"And all she's seen me do is sit here in this chair, in this place. Does that make sense to anyone?"

I'm glad she didn't turn to me for an answer.

"Next time she visits, I'm going to hold her on my lap, right Sami? Just like I'm holding you. I'm going to tell her a story. Any story. I have lots of them. That's something I know how to do. I don't need to read."

Lucia looked away. "And to hell with Socorro! Next time she tells me that I screwed up my kids' lives, I'm going to remind her of this!"

She placed the well-loved page on my lap.

"Can you read this for me?"

It was a crayon-scribbled note in an adult's hand, and a picture of a mother and daughter with fingerless hands touching, in front of a house with a flat roof. The drawing had the disproportion of a four-year-old's eye. The mother held a bundle, and there were several pale blue triangles in the background. The Sisters.

The dark and solitude of the prison compressed us into tight, shadowy spaces we often didn't care to face. It made us crave light. Lucia hadn't earned a hug, but I sure as hell thought she would appreciate one. I would do that one day, but for now, I touched the note gently and told her what she wanted to hear.

"It says 'I am waiting for you. Your loving daughter, Noelia.'"

CASE NOTES VIII

As I understand the story, a group of solidary women friends defied Tony's orders to the contrary and brought Russell in for testimony just before that last weekend. Tony, the consular agent and Russell's lawyer had wanted Russell close, to sign some new agreement they had cooking: nothing that our lawyer knew about specifically. But the judge had clearly made an opening for new testimony to provide evidence of our innocence, and Tomas listed Russell as the first witness. Russell was to testify, as was the highest town official – who had little direct input on the case, but I suppose they wanted someone "ranking" to make the point. After all, the movements were scripted by the university. They just needed to get the proper pieces in place so the file would read well under scrutiny.

I continued scribbling in my notebook, but I changed the tone of my musings. I started writing text for thank yous: for Bill to post on the "freetheoaxacathree" website he had mastered, for the many letters I would be writing when we got out. Against all logic, I was thinking positive. I wrote Concha a poem, about a hummingbird nest I found once, made with fur from my Persian cat. Something about the soft parts inside, and bringing the "enemy" in close... I gave Susa the last of my Hershey's kisses. She wasn't going to give up her habit, and I knew she could sell them, enjoy them, or use the foil. I took stock of what I had left to distribute to the rest: crackers, oatmeal, cookies, nuts, dried fruit. Lemon-flavored potato chips. Some homemade dill bread from a friend who baked amazing things (one of the few things I was reluctant to share). I had eaten the last of her miracle bars. Miracle Bars! What an ironic name for a treat in prison.

Any possible release was still days away -- days that strung out long and lean and noisy in front of me. But this time, Russell had spoken to the judge. And I trusted the strength of his testimony, as well as what looked like the ultimate surrender of the mechanism that would keep us falsely imprisoned. The university had wearied under the pressure of so much truth. It would seem that the unrelenting squeeze tactics brought to bear by a circle of friends forged of toughest steel, as well as the press, the State Department, and lawyers – had convinced the university that we were more dangerous to them in, than out.

ANA

*"We are free, truly free, when we don't need to rent our arms to anybody
in order to be able to lift a piece of bread to our mouths."*
Ricardo Flores Magón (1874-1922)

Two black dial phones rang all day on a long table, a rough wooden cubicle fashioned like a confessional around each to simulate privacy. The worn panels surrounding the phones were rutted with doodles and names of loved ones engraved with the weight of frustration and a ballpoint pen. The surface had been sanded several times, forming a palimpsest where new names intertwined with dates long past.

Pinche Payaso   5 febrero bye bye   mea culpa

Once a day I sat inside the cubicle, at a low stool, alone with my caller for five minutes. Plugging one ear with a finger, and the other with the heavy black receiver, the rage of shouts ricocheting against metal against concrete then back against themselves, fell away to a dull ache. Through the wizardry of connection that had more to do with will than with fiber optics, callers could hear only my voice; I could hear only theirs.

In the small dark room just inside the entry gate to the men's courtyard, these two phones received all incoming calls for 1300 prisoners, men and women. Between the hours of ten a.m. and five p.m. Daily including Sundays.

"Penitenciaria de Ixcotel... Un momento."

The operator on duty scribbled the name of the prisoner requested to an assistant who called over the loudspeaker.

"Rafael Buendia, telephone call! Rafael Buendia, *llamada telefónica!*"

The men who heard and knew where he was—in the kitchen, sweeping, boxing, sleeping—took up the shout.

"Rafa! Your mother's calling!"

"Your mamaciiiiita!"

"Hurry, man!"

"Rafael Buendiiiiiia!"

Rafael Buendia arrived, breathless, to receive his call, as the operator couldn't hold the phone long given there were only two.

When a call came in for a woman prisoner, a runner was dispatched, and the caller was instructed to ring back in twenty minutes. It was not an easy trick for anyone to get through to one of these two phones once, and getting through twice was a feat of true patience. My friend Maureen called every day. Every day! My reprieve from the sitting, the sitting, the sitting. It was my only time to walk, sometimes unaccompanied, in the passageway between the men's and women's sides. Seven minutes if I walked slowly, but I usually hurried to calls. Nobody counted. I often received several calls a day from friends or family patient enough to call and call again. They left me with a buoyant feeling, with fine shavings of freedom from thirty or so fleeting minutes outside of the compound, and the beauty of the thin, bright voices on the end of the line that didn't know these walls.

Ana received daily calls, too, and often we coincided. We both worked the operators, making small talk with them as we waited for our callback to come. Ana was flirty.

"Hey, handsome! Waiting for me?"

I was more... sisterly.

"You from Yucatan? I think I recognize that accent."

We were both effective. Inside, people were more interested in letting down walls than in putting up new ones. After a time the operators didn't keep track of our five minutes, and wouldn't rap on the confessional wall for us to hang up unless somebody waiting in line complained.

It was in that line waiting for our callbacks that Ana and I started to talk. She seemed to know everyone, as if she had been here for years. But if she had been here for years, she wouldn't be sleeping, as she was, in the far corner of the *cacahuate* with us. I leaned against the wall waiting for my call to come in one day, and she bounced in, zapping the air in that dark space with a ray of good cheer.

"Hey, Ana! Here, I saved this for you, *mi reina*."

The assistant who announced the names on the loudspeaker gave her a droopy golden weed that he pulled out of the back pocket of his jeans.

"Oooooh, Joaquín!" She took the strange bloom as if it were a prized orchid. "But what would your *wife* think?" and she winked and exaggeratedly touched her cheek, bowing her head as if she were blushing. The other guys around elbowed each other and smirked.

"My wife! Hah! I taught her a long time ago not to be jealous. Besides, unless she's up there sleeping with the Director, she's not seeing what these cameras are seeing!"

Joaquín's laugh was cut short.

"Eutimio Flores! Call for Eutimio Flores!"

"Time to work, *guapa*—see ya later!"

"Hope it's soon!" Ana gave him a seductive wave and moved toward the line. A tall man just leaving made a sweeping gesture with his arm, as if throwing his coat across a puddle for her to take her place behind me in line. She had that effect.

You couldn't say that too many of the women in Ixcotel dazzled, but Ana did. Always made up and accessorized, her expressive lips were sometimes cranberry, sometimes melon. Her dimpled and freckled cheeks, and that shock of curly black hair were a frame for unguarded huntress eyes, luminous and strangely serious in the midst of her circus of color.

She manicured her orchid pink nails to show off slender fingers, grooved where she once wore many rings that were now sealed in a plastic bag somewhere awaiting her release. Her clothes were lively and provocative, never pants, always a plummeting V. You couldn't miss her. And you couldn't miss her confidence.

And I couldn't imagine that she actually felt comfortable in the confinement of Ixcotel, though the poise with which she moved could have been mistaken for ease. I had once seen a scarlet macaw in a cage, pulling bright feathers through its magnificent beak, first shiny cobalt from the tips of its wings, then saffron, and slowly, languidly the ruby shoulders. He chattered away happily to himself. It was impossible to believe that the bright bird felt enough solace in its own beauty to stop yearning for the dappled shade of the rainforest. Yet so he made it seem.

"So you get calls every day, too, I see." She opened the conversation, sticking the golden weed behind her ear and fluffing her curls.

"Yeah, from a really good friend." Maureen called with news about what the network of friends was putting together on the outside to help get me out. I had people who visited every day. I had friends who brought food and water. I had folks who could bring me clean clothes, international reporters and endless telephone cards. Nobody else inside had this kind of ceaselessly visible support, and I doubted that anyone had as strong a movement on the outside to set the wheels rolling for their release.

"I get my calls every day from the movement." Ana pulled a stray thread from the hem of her skirt.

"The movement?" Maybe I was wrong.

"Yeah, I work with a human rights association in the Mixteca region. I was just a secretary, filing and stuff, but I have my law degree."

The Mixteca region was far away in mist and mountains. I couldn't place Ana there.

"You didn't want to practice law?" I thought she would be a great lawyer—she certainly knew how to get people to open, how to make connections.

"Oh, I would have practiced law, but it had to be good law. My father and brother are drive-a-big-car lawyers, and they lost sight of things." Ana pulled a small compact from a pouch slung across her chest and looked into the tiny mirror, pursing her lips and arranging her curly bangs across her forehead as if preparing for a photo shoot.

"What things did they lose sight of?" It looked like we were going to have plenty of time to ask questions, as our calls weren't coming through.

"What my grandfather taught us. My father got out of the *campo* as soon as he could. He thought the city would teach us more than that red corner of earth where my grandfather taught."

"Your grandfather was a teacher?"

"Oh, not really. He wasn't a teacher in a school or anything. He was a farmer. But he was always teaching us. Things that matter more than law school."

"You really admire him."

"He is the reason I take each hard step I do, the only man I have ever loved. Except for this big guy doling out the phone calls!"

Ana's change of humor kept me at full attention, as she turned to the operator to check on her call.

"Hey there, handsome. You sure nothing's come in for me yet? I've been waiting a year now."

"I'll let you know, dark eyes."

"Don't forget me now!"

"Can a drowning man forget his life raft?"

Ana turned back to me and said "I think he just compared me to an over-inflated piece of rubber!" And she giggled but he didn't hear because he was picking up his next call. Ana, adjusting her sleeveless blouse to cover her bra strap, picked up again.

"So I started working at the human rights organization where my grandfather lives. Drove my father and brother nuts. 'Why the hell did you study law to do this?'" Ana shook her head, as we do sometimes at a naughty pup too cute to scold.

"Anyway, there I was, helping with writing letters and stuff, and then *Zas!*"

"*Zas?*" Ana's unfolding story was intriguing. Up until this time, I hadn't yet met an activist with pink nails.

"Yeah, *Zas!* Wham! I end up here! Turned out the governor thought that our work there was… I don't know… threatening."

"The governor put you in jail?"

"Oh yeah, *nuestro estimado gobernador!* Very sweet. Me and my *compañeros.* He called us in one day to talk about the land and our corn. We thought he was making an opening to talk, really talk. I was just going to take notes. And *Órale!*"

"*Órale?*"

"Yeah, *Órale!* Next thing I know we were ushered into an unmarked black pickup with tinted windows, no plates, and a thug for a driver. Mirrored sunglasses and the whole works. Only thing missing was a scar on his cheek. We ended up here."

"So you're a political prisoner?"

"Is that what you'd call me? I don't know…"

She stopped to wave at a guy in the courtyard where the four p.m. shift was starting to sweep.

"My two *compañeros* have been in a few times before. It's no big deal, they say."

"No big deal, right." It felt like a big deal to me. I wondered if she was buying it.

"There's a whole bunch of people working the system on the outside for our release. A few of us get thrown in each month. I've been here three months so far, but I should be out soon. Meanwhile, we've got people coming with signs every day to picket outside!"

She stopped here, pensive, and removed one golden hoop earring. She ran it over her lips playfully, then placed it around three fingers of her right hand, raising it as if making a pact.

"I was a sec-re-tary. C'mon. A nobody. Okay, a nobody with a law degree, but still on the waiting list for real action. Now my name is in the newspapers. Not that I wanted to be famous, but if this publicity gives the movement a better chance to expose the reason we end up in here, it's worth it. I swear on my golden earring, your honor."

"What *is* the reason, Ana? That reason you want to expose?" I wanted to know what could make her incarceration "worth it."

She put the hoop back into her ear and raised her eyebrows at me, fussing with the earring, apparently to give herself time to think, as she straightened like an orator.

"Just take a look. You've seen it. Turns out that on the outside none of us are really free, are we?" and she shook her head as we do sometimes when we are facing a hill that we know will tire us of breath before we reach the top.

"Free speech? You think we have it? Free will? Free education? Free kick in the gut, that's what we got. It's a different kind of captivity out there, sure—depending on the kind of floor you wash every day. Dirt or marble. But we're all captives of something. Or someone. Or some place. We don't always see it, though."

She bent down to adjust the strap on her heels. "That's another thing I learned from my *abuelito*."

And she changed the subject, not giving me time to make sense of her metaphors, though I could see she had a riff going on injustice and inequality. As anyone might who had poked around in the margins of Mexico.

"Hey, who are your *compañeros* here on the men's side?" She kept to a trail pretty well.

"Oh, they were neighbors. We all happened to be living on the same plot of land outside of Oaxaca, and one night they just—" and we were cut short by Ana's incoming call.

"Hey, Ana—it's your other boyfriend!"

"Yeah, the one who takes me out to dinner, which *you've* never done, Mr. Shipwreck!" And Ana winked at me, making a little circle in the air with her finger which meant "later!" She ducked into the cubicle, took the receiver, plugged one ear with her finger, and closed her eyes.

I guess Maureen couldn't get through that day. I stayed leaning against the wall watching everyone else's calls come in, watching the operator's lips willing him to say "Maria Elena!" If nobody came for me, I would stand there until five pm. At least I wasn't sitting, sitting, sitting, sitting in the courtyard. And here I got to almost hear one side of some very interesting conversations.

I wondered if it was easier to do the time, to wake up to the shouts of the guard tower, to slog through the days and endure the stone floor nights, the noise, the tedium of waiting, the noise, the noise, and more than anything not knowing— was it easier, if you thought the whole, brutal, angular, screaming metallic mess was "worth it" for a cause you believed in? I wanted to think so for Ana. But still, she didn't choose to be within the walls of Ixcotel to prove her point. And what point was she proving? That might does not make right? That you can't take away the things that matter? That enough is enough? The bywords of popular movements that were written on placards like the ones paraded in front of the jail to beg for her release, had been shouted in dozens of languages: YA BASTA! STOP ALREADY! The oppressors didn't shout back. They placed their jangling gold coins in soft pouches and manipulated a system that came close to making innocence a requirement for being inside the screeching prison doors. So Ana, a sec-re-tary whose crime was choosing the right place to work—was it easier for her? She was one of the few who felt pretty enough to polish her nails, but she still had to change her tampon in a bathroom without privacy, like the rest of us.

At five-fifteen I headed to the women's compound in time for roll call, before anyone could come to haul me back. I walked slowly, reciting a rhyme with each step from second year Spanish Conversation class. The professor had us memorize rhymes for diction, relating stories about her former students who were prisoners of war and repeated the rhymes to keep themselves from disappearing. I paced it out eleven times before I arrived back at the courtyard.

En este mundo traidor step step step *nada es verdad ni mentira.* step step *Todo es según el color* step step step *del cristal con que se mira.* step step

— In this traitorous world, nothing is false or true. Everything is tinted by the lens we're looking through. —

Three wash tubs lined up against the wall opposite the entrance to the bathroom. Besides the kitchen where the usuals claimed the stove and sinks, the tubs were the only place we had ready access to running water. From early morning and ceaselessly on through the day, they were used for washing clothes, though anyone using the one on the end had to make space for women who wanted to wash their hands, brush their teeth or rinse their *rancho* plate. The next day as I arrived to brush my teeth, I ran into Ana at this third tub, twisting the soapy water from her panty hose. I wanted to hear more of her story—the rebel lawyer practicing the things that matter in a far-off corner of red earth. With a mouthful of toothpaste I said through my brush, to sound casual, "Ana, what does your family think of you stuck in here?"

"Oh, they're pretty distressed. My father wanted to get the best lawyers on it because he's sure I've been raped and cattle prodded, but the organization has its own lawyers who know how to do this. My brother kinda said 'See?' and my grandfather… he´s planting corn. Even though the rainy season is over. My father thinks he's crazy, but grandpa says 'You watch—it'll send up a shoot.'"

"I like your grandfather."

A lot of people thought we were beaten or given rats for dinner or worse. My own friends and family accused me of hiding the truth from them, that surely there was blood or starvation involved. Bleak? Ixcotel was bleak—but much of our daily existence there was darkened solely by the simple, unavoidable and immutable fact that we simply couldn't leave. A manipulated justice system said we could not decide to do something different. We could not choose to go somewhere that better suited us.

"Just about everybody who works with these causes has done some time. They got a whole bunch of us after the snake incident."

I was careful not to spit my toothpaste out on her laundry. "What snake?"

"The frog-eating snakes of the resistance." She said this slowly, as we do sometimes when we are telling a parable, each word weighted with soon-to-be-unfurled moral significance.

"I don't get it." Her metaphors were showing again.

"When the Mixteca went to the city last April to see the legislators about the bioengineered corn that had been documented up there after that big study from *Berquelee*, our fine lawmakers wouldn't open the doors. I wasn't there, that's just what I heard."

Berquelee. Ana knew of the University of California study that found genetically modified corn in remote regions of Oaxaca. Freckles and dimples and brains.

"So you guys help organize the Mixteca?"

Ana laughed. "Oh, they are already pretty organized. I guess they've been organized for thousands of years more than we have, so it's not like we can teach them anything! It's done by consensus there, same as it has been for centuries, so good organization was natural for them. Sort of organic. Communal lands, communal decisions—a kind of primal socialism." Ana stopped to gather her hose in a tight ball, wrapping it in a yellow terry cloth towel.

Ana was bright and illuminating, and had lived in the indigenous zones that I had grown to respect. I wanted to understand her trust that her situation would work out. I was still struggling with the realization that presumption of guilt had survived here for so long. She was lucky to have a grandfather who rooted her to the earth. Trust in cycles could help with these impossible-seeming things.

Ana rolled a plastic bag into a tight ball to plug the tub and to keep the soapy water in. She continued, either sensing my interest, or from her own. It's not like we had anywhere else to go.

"So if anything, they organize us! We just help them take their decisions to where they can be heard, facilitate lawyers, that kind of thing. You know they feel that if their corn is compromised, impure, their whole culture is in danger. They believe our race comes from corn. I guess it's no stranger than being spawned from a spontaneously generated couple wearing fig leaves."

Ana's voice was calm, but she was picking furiously at one tapered pink nail that had begun to chip.

"So what's this about the snakes, Ana?"

"Oh, yeah, the snakes. It was a kick. So these people traveled to the capital to talk about a law to protect the purity of their corn, like I said. And the lawmakers didn't let them in. They peeked out the doors of the legislative palace, saw people in sarapes and sombreros, and shook their heads. Again, I wasn't there, but I know how these things go."

Ana pulled a lacy mint green nightshirt and a black satiny bathrobe from her laundry bag. Her story had my full attention, but I was equally as amazed watching her wardrobe unfurl. I slept in my clothes, and others slept in sweats and tee shirts or housedresses. She must have seen the grin at the corners of my eyes, and said, "Hey, it's only as prison as you make it, my friend!"

"So the folks from the *sierra*, they just camped out on the steps, waiting. Eating tortillas and bread and drinking coffee. As the day wore on and they were told over and over to wait, nobody's in to receive them, in another hour, you know—well, they decided to use Plan B. Always have a Plan B. I learned that from them. They opened up their bags and emptied loads of frog-eating snakes and big ugly rats through the open windows into the offices!"

"You're kidding." It was almost too good to be real.

"No, for real! Creative, huh? Don't cross the oppressed! The snakes weren't poisonous or anything. Not that anyone in the offices knew that for sure! They said a man fainted!"

"Did they let the group in?"

"Ohhhhhh yeah! And as you could guess, nothing has changed yet with their corn. But they have some more tricks up their sleeve—a play they want to perform in the streets."

She gathered her nightie and robe, and her plastic bottle of laundry soap, and was off to read a beauty magazine on the rooftop space where she hung her clothes to dry in the sun. She stayed close to them, not trusting her nighties to be out of her sight.

Ana came back from the phone cubicles that afternoon, elated. She told me she was pretty sure she was about to get out. I was happy for her, but familiar with the shifts and sways of getting closer to the door. This business of release was a tricky one. For those of us who had active cases, lawyers who were present and really working, each weekend brought the possibility of a change in the wind. I wasn't comfortable talking about it to most of the women, as some rarely saw their lawyer. Even with Ana I gave non-specific answers. "They're hopeful." "Looks good." "Maybe soon." Every weekend new hoops to jump, a new negotiation, a new testimony— and every Monday, sometimes Tuesday, the curtain fell. *Yes... yes... yes... yes, hang on there... almost... Ohhhh, sorry.* Ana trusted her one pure link to the outside world—her daily phone calls—and her contacts told her it was time.

"And just in time, too, as my *abuelito* isn't doing too well. He was bitten by a *chintatlahua*."

A black widow.

"Is he okay?"

"My father says he still hobbled out to talk to that little mound where he planted the corn. Sounds fine to me! He's been bitten lots of times. Tough old guy."

"When will you know about your release, Ana?"

"Tomorrow! I'm going to wear yellow! I'm going straight from here to *abuelo's* house. He says yellow is the color of freedom.

Freedom means a lot to him. He used to tell us about the Flores Magon brothers—I think he knew them."

"The revolutionaries?"

"Yeah. Them. My *abuelito* was all about the land and freedom—proud to be a farmer."

"I'm glad you'll be with him soon."

It's not like we could stay in "bed." The next day I was up to sweep at dawn. Even if we managed to sleep through the blare of the guard tower at six a.m., the other women sweepers knew who needed to be out there helping, and we would get a nudge. Not a "good morning," just a nudge. We were communal and solidary with each other in Ixcotel, but nonsensical niceties fell away. There were few really good mornings anyway. The guards were cheery, though -- the only ones who would brave a "good morning," but at least someone did.

Ana had bought brooms when she first came in, earning an extra hour to sleep while we cleaned the courtyard. But at 7:30, there was roll call, and heaven help the woman who wasn't dressed, present and identifiable. I had seen Ana at the outgoing pay phones earlier when we swept, then she disappeared.

She wasn't present at roll call. When her name was called, the boss lady said "Infirmary!" and the guards made a tick on their sheets. Damn. Sick on the day of her release! I didn't believe anything till it happened... but optimism was a reflex for me, even if I tried to keep hope in a sane and logical place. I really wanted to see her get out, today!

When I went into the *cacahuate* to get a pen from the bag where I stored my stuff, I saw Ana sitting slumped in a chair in front of the television, nervously biting her nails. She had bitten her nails and stripped her polish clean, leaving flecks of pink like drops of blood on her yellow skirt.

I didn't want to interrupt her thoughts. She seemed intent, though not in her usual way. Nobody else was around, so I offered her a cracker from what my friends brought the day before.

"No, not now."

"You okay?"

"Not really." Her voice was low and heavy, like a soaking fog.

"I heard you were in the infirmary."

"Yeah." I could barely hear her.

"Anything you want to talk about?"

"No, not really." Maybe she mumbled this, or maybe I knew from the shake of her head. I walked away and kept an eye on her from a distance.

She sat as the TV crowd built around her. They changed the stations and laughed at the silly shows, and Ana sat. Once she stood up to brush the flakes of polish from her skirt, and she moved her chair back into a corner.

"Ana Saldaño! *Sale Libre*! Release!" The guard's voice rang out, calling for Ana to appear to sign her release papers. I was under the pomegranate tree—the birds weren't fluttering and cooing as they usually did when a release was coming up.

"Ana Saldaño!" Again they called for her.

"I'll get her!"

I walked into the daytime darkness of the *cacahuate* where the TV blared. With only small windows at the top for air circulation, the room stayed cool in the day, but dark like a protected grotto. A grotto full of jaundiced, hypnotized women painted by the techno glow from a television whose realistic colors had long ago given way to garish oranges and yellows.

"Ana? They're calling you to go."

"I know." She didn't raise her eyes, but I saw they were closed. I heard her take a deep breath. The tint from the TV was at the top of her head, on her curly hair that hadn't yet been combed by more than her ragged fingers. Yellow-for-freedom she had said.

"C'mon, Ana. What's wrong?"

"It's like we're in a deep well and we can see the sunlight at the top, but we can't scale up the walls, they're slick with slime. We can hear their voices calling. Maybe they drop a blanket down. But we can't get to them. I feel more captive today than the day I walked in."

"Ana, but they called you to sign your release papers! Didn't you hear them?"

"Yeah, I heard them. Sign my release from one captivity to another. I'll leave in two hours, and go to my *abuelo's* house to close his eyes and cover his face with a yellow sarape. Plan B. The *chintatlahua* won."

"Oh, Ana…"

"Yeah. He would have loved this one. The little guy kicks the big guy's ass."

I walked Ana to the guard's gate, from where she was escorted to the judge's chambers to sign her release papers. She returned in a half hour or so, still sullen. She went to her space on the shelf, and everyone gathered around.

"I'll take the sandals, Ana!"

"Shut up, Susa! You get everything! Leave some for the rest of us!"

"Me! Me! I need toothpaste!"

Ana was dutifully distributing what was left of her belongings—tradition as a woman left. She was as spirited as she could muster—the face she wanted to give the crowd.

"And who'll take this bottle of pretty pink polish?"

And she threw it like a bride's bouquet into the crowd, as too many "Me's!" and too many arms reached for her at the same time.

She came up to me just before she left. She was golden—her yellow skirt, white top and a sleek band the color of daffodils holding the curls back from her face. Her eyes were bright. Not quite a total transformation: her nails were still ragged and unpainted, and there was a somber tilt to her lips.

"You'll be out soon, too. Hang in there."

"Yeah, good luck, Ana."

"Luck? I think what we need is creativity, Mari. Inside, there's one way to work it. Well, two if you happen to have a judge who can be bought. But out there, our future captivity? A thousand ways we can fight it. I've got my money on frog-eating snakes."

MARI SALE LIBRE

Release

We expected the news to come Monday, after our fourth weekend. But on Sunday, November 9, Tomas called for me from the men's compound. I rushed over, unaccompanied. By now the guards were tired of my frequent legal visits, and told me just to stay clear of the warden. John hadn't arrived yet. Tomas gave me a thumbs up sign from about ten paces. This was the second time I cried in Ixcotel.

For 33 nights I unrolled a yoga mat in my assigned space on the floor in the *cacahuate*, three tiles wide, and wondered if that night would be my last dreaming of home with the women of Ixcotel. I was released on the evening of a lunar eclipse.

I wondered what I would say at the end, to the women who chiseled this improbable community into such an inhospitable landscape, the women who handed me tools to work alongside them. *This is how we work in Ixcotel. This is how we love. This is how we grieve and hope and spit on the ground in Ixcotel. This is how we make it through a day.*

What would I say?

"*Gracias*" would be like more watered-down coffee; a whiff of appreciation, then it would fall miserably short. What would I say to the women who reached to me every day because we were different, because we were the same? Once, five women stood with me at the phone to sing "Happy Birthday" in Spanish to Bill's answering machine, at 7am just after our morning sweep. Once, a woman gave me a pair of plastic sandals because she saw me standing barefoot in the shower. Once, a woman came to me to cry, saying she didn't want her daughter, who slept alongside us, to know that she was losing hope. *"Pretend we are discussing something important."* And she let me take her hand. Once, a visiting father entrusted me to remind his daughter to eat. Once a visiting daughter drew lions and lilies in my notebook. Once I lived in Ixcotel, with a community of ex-communicated women who insisted daily through stitches on napkins, through curses and prayers, through filling lines in a blank notebook—that we would not lose to the dark, that part of us that quickened at the reminder of birdsong from the towering trees outside the barbed wire.

During the roll call where I intoned, for the final time, the creed of "I am here" with the women of Ixcotel, the guard announced my departure. I had not heard this done before. *"Mari sale libre."* The hoots and whistles, claps and cheers made me blush. The woman who came in right after me and fell into formation behind me each day, said "I hope I'm next."

Susa asked for special permission to walk me to the gate to help me carry my bedding and clothes. I reached to hug her, and she gave me a thumbs-up sign. "You're on your own now," she said. Indeed.

"Gracias, Susa." It was all I could say.

Reunited with John and Joe at the exit, uniformed officers asked us to repeat our names and birth dates to confirm that they were releasing the correct prisoners. They pushed open a wall-high metal gate that groaned as if it had not been opened in years. Our friends, all arms, waited just outside with Tomas. In the bit of moonlight that remained before it went dark, freedom shone citrus-bright, like sunrays on lemons. I squinted as we do sometimes when first awakening.

UNTIL IT'S TIME TO COME BACK

From Oaxaca to New York

I left Mexico ten days after my release. I followed the steps laid out for me. Airplane ticket to New York City provided by my former employer. Sweaters for fall provided by friends. Space to sleep provided by Bill.

I went to Casa Ames by day and packed books in boxes to be gifted, sent or donated to the local library, though I slept at a friend's house, deciding not to test the will of the university regarding my presence on the land. I thanked everyone who stopped by the house, and they were many. I took long looks at the mountains that had safeguarded me for three years, green in that season, alive and silent. I said goodbye. This time, none of the delicately weighed and staunchly solid decision that characterized other big shifts in my life was present. It was like sitting in the dentist's chair. Nothing hurt--I was numb. I garbled responses to questions, my tongue lazy and my mouth full of ineffective, misshapen words. I felt myself slipping off to that other place I go when I sit for a root canal. Nothing hurts, but nothing is pleasant, so I exit. In my head I play in the sea a bit, or buy fresh tortillas and chat with the vendors in the colorful morning market until it's time to come back, or until the Novocain wears off. After prison, I took the steps that everyone else thought I should take, because for the first time in three decades of assertive independence, I had no opinion. I was numb.

When it was time to say goodbye to Russell, the sorrow in my chest cut clean through the fog, yet the control I had mustered while in prison kept me from crying. It kept me from speaking, too—the knot of words I would have said plugged the emotions: deep-set and for the moment invisible. I met Russell's eyes and touched my heart where sorrow struggled, mute. I didn't need words to be understood. He said "You have been through a lot."

I arrived in New York City and Bill was at the airport with flowers and a hug. I had reverse metamorphosed in the silver chrysalis of that jet from Mexico to New York. I became a caterpillar. I didn't know how caterpillars expressed happiness, or sadness, or grief. I hugged Bill back, pretending for the moment to be happy. Maybe I was, but it felt too much like sadness.

Two weeks after arriving in New York, 24 nights after release from Ixcotel, I dreamed of my dog, Nini. I left her and my two beloved cats in Oaxaca, as there was no space for pets in Bill's small Upper East Side apartment. Cats are adaptable—I told them I'd be back soon and they blinked and walked off. But dogs... dogs are different. Their concept of home is twined with scents and people, with companions and the reassuring routine of everyday. They're not happy just anywhere. Fortunately, Nini was adopted by good friends and went to a house just down the road, where we had spent a lot of time together. She would be loved and in a familiar place.

But in my dream Nini was lost, running between our houses on the dirt road that joined them. Wet black nose to the ground, she tracked a scent, uprooted rocks, snuffed at leaves. She whined and tested the wind for traces of the life she remembered. No one called to her. No one knew her name. She recognized nothing. She was achingly tired and wanted to settle herself down to sleep, but couldn't find home.

It was the first time I cried, really cried, since the night in holding when the lawyer didn't show. I left bed and sobbed in the bathroom, my shoulders shaking, my naïve hope that everything would be okay, shaking too. I cried for Nini, for me, for home.

When I first entered Ixcotel, several women asked if I was Mexican. Certainly not because I looked Mexican but rather, they said, because I didn't cry. They thought that only a Mexican could understand that disquiet, disquieting place. Mexico had been my home for 17 years. And while I didn't profess to understand her, I had chosen her precisely because she tested me, and I grew to love her for the cracks in her sidewalks, grew to learn from the way she resettles after a quake. I had studied the dance, two steps forward, one step back. Yet here in New York, I lost count. I might have stepped back three, four, cinco, seis. In New York, its sidewalks unbroken and aligned, my Mexican ability to scale pyramids and settle back after the earth trembled had no place to roost. And then, anything I had learned about balance and acceptance was spent in Ixcotel.

Still, I invented a new story, imagining wings: My home near Central Park is warmly receptive. With an intelligent and mature new partner, we face some tough decisions together with a growing sense of intimate partnership. I am connected, yet free. That extraordinary joy in freedom, not experienced by most people who have not suffered its absence, buoys me through the trials of readjustment to a new life in a new country. I re-toggle my experience and devote my energies to a worthy, well-paying cause, and delight in the diversity and challenge of New York. I am, after all, accustomed to radical change, to seismic shifts and rumbles.

During the first two weeks before the dream of Nini soaked me in displacement metaphor, all of that seemed possible. Anything seemed possible. Twenty one baby possums fit in a matchbox. Innocent women sleep nose to nose on the floor. I become a New Yorker.

Bill set aside drawer space and my family prepared Thanksgiving dinner, inviting television cameras in to film the local woman's homecoming. I spent hours writing thank-yous by hand on blue note paper to the pack of friends and supporters who followed our journey and unquestioningly threw their voices and resources behind us. Bill taught me subway etiquette—don't hug the pole--and the logical grid of the city, and we ate Burmese rice and Baba Ganouj along Second Avenue. We decided not to define where our relationship would go, only to note where it was at the time, and to nurture and water its shoot-green freshness, assuring its exposure to sunlight. Neither one of us could make much commitment beyond that, but it was enough.

I was uncharacteristically, undeniably and fully dependent. And I was not yet home.

After the dream, the tears didn't stop for a long time. I was in a Garcia-Marquez tale, filling the house with tears. They stained the walls and watered the plants. We used them for cooking pasta and for mopping the floor when winter came inside. I wrung them from the sheets. They splashed onto our toes with a plinking sound. They froze on my cheeks on my morning walks through the park and I kept my head down so people wouldn't see. The neighbors complained that my tears streamed down two stories of ceiling, onto their collection of jazz CD's. I just didn't stop crying.

When I was a child I had a set of Colorforms. Plastic backgrounds, one a sea, one a forest, one a house—and I moved the flat pink girl with her plastic wardrobe from world to world. She adhered by static cling and never lost her smile. I carefully peeled her from the forest to the house at the end of her day. In New York, I was suddenly pasted on a background I did not recognize. I didn't know who was around me on the street, or what they did all day. I didn't recognize half of what they sold in the grocery store, 10 varieties of pickle, 15 of fabric softener. Engulfed by the crowd, I was a sandaled bumpkin in the posh Upper East Side where women dressed in furs and walked diamond-collared Chihuahuas who were better dressed than I for winter, sporting tiny and fashionably appropriate boots and caps. I looked out over the mosaic of windows that tiled the night landscape, and was shaken by the anonymity of a place where in one sweeping glance I could touch thousands of lives with my gaze, yet know no one. I didn't know basic things, like how to walk on a New York street. Bill tried to teach me to just walk straight, don't hesitate, but I yielded. I stalled. I crawled. I thought New Yorkers had the right of way over me, the newcomer, the outsider, the alien. I saw immigrants on the subway platform, faces I recognized as Mexican. I wanted to ask them how they could bear the cold, the amorphous crowds, how did they bear the lack of trilling r's. How did they adhere to this new background? I wanted to know their secret for adjustment. I looked like I belonged, but I carried the heavy bags of an immigrant.

I was angry at everyone. I built a career on being a Professionally Pleasant Person, but couldn't set up a phone contract without a struggle of wills. I was angry at Bill for being himself. Steady, sure, unflinching, unflappable Bill. I was angry at myself for being none of those things, for having lost my core of calm. I was angry because I was out and the women weren't, and I was crying and they might be crying too, but they had reason. I was angry at the taxis that honked and the trains that squealed and the booted dogs, the people with jobs and homes, I was angry at winter then angrier at spring. Spring! How dare she come now and pour out flirty blooms and hope when I am dry and dormant still? I was angry at magnolias. I wanted to will them back into their buds, back into the bark, back into an unseen place where they are about to be beautiful. I was not ready for them.

I thought a job would orient me. I worked piecemeal on subtitles and translation when interview after interview flattened my cocky assurance that a good job would come quickly. I sat for hours and listened, rewound, cried, typed, forwarded through episodes of "This Old House" and "DIY Home Improvement" learning carpentry terms like bird's mouth and cat's paw. This brought in next-to-nothing as I was not good at it, my attention span short and my tedium threshold low after the round-the-clock boredom of prison. I knew I wanted to work in non-profit after emptying my energies into the corporate world for so long, but I needed specific skills. I went to training sessions on fund raising and grant writing, convincing myself that my hour-long course could help me compete with the scores of people with experience in New York—because I had desire. I liked interviewing—it was a connection. And I was often called back for second interviews and thirds. But in the end, there was always a candidate with the precise qualifications, no need for bending, and I fell back into the pool of seekers.

Or maybe some of my cloud was discernable at interviews. Things weren't getting better. I recalled having down times in Mexico, when I would flip through the calendar a month and draw a smile on a random day, assuring myself that by the time that date came around, I'd be smiling again. And it worked. By drawing a smile, I practiced my deep-rooted optimism and lifted myself out of sadnesses, some not so small. I learned in New York, though, the logarithmic difference between sadness and depression as I flipped through months of the calendar with no change. Four months into the cascade of tears, I admitted I needed help. I was weary of not recognizing myself, not knowing how to get inside or get outside, how to turn anything on or off.

A friend I've known for decades used to say if his plane was going down he would want me by his side, because my inner calm was unshakable. I think this was a compliment of sorts at the time, though it sounded a bit like a shared death-wish. In the pulsing cityscape of New York where I was forced to face my very naked, squirming ego—unprotected by a professional identity, by my story, without a gaggle of friends around me, without purpose, roots, a home, isolated without my adopted language—my name suddenly returned to its birth form after seventeen years of musicality--without accomplishments, without Mexico, without independence, without me—I was afraid of the dark that I found, afraid to face it and discover that I may not find hope there. I was shaken to have to meet who I was and who I wasn't anymore.

The phone is heavy in my hand. I recall another phone, the curled metal cord. In Ixcotel.

There is a small stone stuck in the ridge of my walking shoes. I remember Concha's sneaker.

I smooth the fabric of my skirt, and I am with Citlali. I can't reach her across the reef.

I touch the articles of my everyday life and they are solid and cool against my fingertips, anchoring, preventing me from falling. My daydreams flash without warning to Ixcotel but I come back, cutting a pear into quarters. A stamp. A ball of lint. A small black bug. A page from Beowulf. A chair... It was an ordinary black office chair that Bill used when he worked on the computer. Just a chair. But in one flash that lasted a millisecond, I didn't recognize the chair or understand how it got there, what part of my reality it inhabited. There seemed to be no meaning to that particular array of molecules. It was as strange to me as I to myself. I suddenly feared more than not knowing who I was or who I wasn't. I feared being in this strange world at all.

I told Bill I was ready to accept his offer to set me up with a therapist. He recommended I call Carole, an upscale Upper East Side talk therapist who charged more per hour than I currently had in the bank. I called because she was a connection—I asked her if she knew someone who worked on a sliding scale. As a favor to Bill I suppose, Carole agreed to see me not once, but twice to start, before she made any recommendations. Those were her rules. I had never been to a therapist and didn't know any rules, so agreed to hers. I didn't know where to sit when I went to her office, warm with calla lilies and hyacinths that made me a little uneasy. That budding again. There were many chairs but I chose to sit alongside her on the leather couch, where our hands could meet and where I was within reach of the box of kleenex. I cried through the first session. And the second. And most subsequent sessions, which were frequent and free (*free!*), for months. Life gave me an angel. Carole was not interested in making money from our therapy. She called me on the telephone between appointments to see how I was doing, tethering me to someone, unexpected, unrequired, who was sure I would get past all this. She was more than a service provider—my dentist fills my tooth and sends me off. Carole went with me when I left her office; she let a kind of love shine through her professional role that reminded me of things I recognized, people helping people. If boundaries were crossed, I'm thankful that she was willing to cross them. Slowly I was re-connecting and becoming less fearful, less angry at the squirming embryo I had unearthed, working instead to do what I would do for any suffering person... put my arm around her and reassure her.

I ached for want of a timeline, though. Even as I breathed deep through the first tear-free days, I lay my head against the cold of the shower stall, wanting to be assured that tomorrow I would stop crying altogether. That this interview would lead to a job the next day. And the day after next, Bill and I would find the key. Not knowing how long the steps would take was eerily familiar and often I woke up facing that prison wall. Yet I was free.

I was free and I saw their faces everywhere on the streets of New York. Full lipped, heavy lidded, high cheeked, drawn, vibrant, painted, wan, changeable faces. Bertha is reading The Wall Street Journal balancing on the A train. And Susa gave up crack and is selling chocolates wrapped in colorful foil, shaped like bunnies for Easter. That woman walking her baby in Central Park looks like Lucia, but her baby would be bigger now. But these are not the women I knew in prison. I want to ask these women: "Can you possibly imagine what it's like not to have a choice? To wake each day to count same hour after same hour? To feel minuscule and helpless against something you cannot control?" But I am afraid. I am afraid they will say "Yes. I know."

Dependence, insecurity, doubt. We wander into other prisons, unaware that we will not slip easily from between their bars.

When I accepted my first full-time position, a low-paying job in a transcription and translation mill, I sent a small taproot into the ground beneath me. I walked out of the office and into a crowd of people who were working, like me. I belonged a little more. I volunteered with a Mexican immigrant support organization to make community that fit with my story. That work turned into another low-paying job. After two years, I met another angel who read between the lines on my resume and offered me an assistant directorship at a non-profit with a long history of strong community service. This one stuck. I made friends and joined writing groups, walking groups. I found more organizations where I could pitch in: prison issues, Hispanic causes. I scratched and scraped to tear through boundaries perceived and real in this city, that by its very grid challenged the part of me that craved the creativity of the broken line. Eventually, I made community and moved to a diverse neighborhood in the north of the city, collected my cats, and gardened in a yard that was sometimes home to raccoons and skunks.

I saw Carole for five years, paying her what I was able as my salary slowly gained momentum, until we both thought it was time.

Eventually I made a new home.

Eventually I found my wings.

I faced the dark and unearthed hope, as Mexico had taught me. I didn't ever find the easy ahh, the flow that I felt in Mexico. But I found enough, for now.

Bill is now one of my best friends. He witnessed facets of me that made me want to run, but I couldn't, and he didn't. We left the romance thing long ago. It was painful to let go—even when a relationship is mismatched, ending it comes with the inevitable laments and tenderness. But we stuck it out and as with so many things, in the ending we found the beginning. We now embrace a permanence forged through fire. Obsidian.

Not long ago, the friends who adopted Nini were in New York with her. We made arrangements to meet, early on a Sunday on the Upper West Side—and we would walk together in Central Park. Nini! I hadn't seen my pup in years. The streets were quiet at that hour. From a block away I saw them. I called to Nini, my friend released the leash, and she came running to me at top speed. I saw the fat puppy who would never be left behind, I saw the square head on my knee as I breathed at our rock, I saw joy. She jumped, she licked, she rolled on her back and then squeezed between my legs. Her joy did not fit in her little dog body. Dogs can express that kind of happiness so much better than humans. I just laughed and hugged her, letting her lick and lick until she was really sure it was me. Once in our lives we shared days. Some wondrous, some dark. Nini had not forgotten, and if her joy was anything like mine, it might have come from the pure delight of one of those singular flashing moments that prove that our lives, twisted and changed as they may become, still contain all their parts.

My experience with prison and the shift it caused in my life left on me an indelible mark. Years after, I am still more prone to tears, particularly at expressions of solidarity, triumph and community. The experience is now part of my life, catalogued with other parts that push me to be where I am, for now, a good place. There are those griefs and gratitudes, like happinesses, carved so deeply into the pyramid of our days, that we have but to lightly run our fingers over the surface to recall. I am never very far from Ixcotel and the women I met there. And Mexico... I got over leaving Mexico, though I may never fully get over living without her. I grope for an impulsive heart that I know lies deep below the surface, trusting that it may suddenly erupt, throwing off sparks that will ignite in me a new accent, restless and uncoiled. I remember Mexico. And I am here now. Taking two steps forward.

Mary Ellen Sanger

EPILOGUE

From Ixcotel toward the horizon

Give the key to the moon to prisoners and the disappointed.
For those who are sentenced to death and for those who are
sentenced to life there is no better tonic than the moon
in precise and regular doses.
— *Jaime Sabines*
(Chiapaneco poet)

October 2013

Fort Collins, Colorado. The autumn is golden, so truly golden
it seems that the very air is charged. I am starting again here. I speak
Spanish with a group of very smart women every Monday. I
volunteer to write with women in the Larimer County Detention
Center and work on campus with diversity initiatives. I make
vindaloo and coconut soup and homemade salsa with Joseph – we
have a very spicy kitchen. And I am discovering life and love in the
foothills of the Rockies.

I love the mountains here, and the moon, and the symmetry
of their origins in the molten heart of the earth. I love seeing far into
the distance now, no walls, and knowing there is mystery there.

I consider myself fortunate, very fortunate.

FOR FURTHER INFORMATION

One of the ways I was able to rebuild community for myself and begin to respond to the work I inherited from the many who supported my cause for release, was through volunteering with the following non-profit and creative causes for justice and freedom of expression. Please take a look and consider supporting one or all if you believe, like I do, that solidarity can be one of the most universal and unambiguous expressions of love.

NY Writers Coalition Inc. (NYWC) provides free creative writing workshops throughout New York City for people from groups that have been historically deprived of voice in our society.

nywriterscoalition.org

I volunteered with NYWC since 2007 as a bilingual workshop leader for New Yorkers who write in Spanish or English.

PEN Prison Writing Program believes in the restorative and rehabilitative power of writing, by providing hundreds of inmates across the country with skilled writing teachers and audiences for their work.

pen.org

I have been a member of the Fiction Committee (responsible for choosing fiction winners in an annual contest) and a member of the general board for the PEN Prison Writing Committee since 2008.

Presumed Guilty, the Movie: Winner of 2010 Emmy Award for Best Investigative Journalism. Released in Mexico in 2011 to great censorship and acclaim, beating "Fahrenheit, 911" as the most-watched documentary in Mexico.

This film was instrumental in bringing the many inconsistencies of the Mexican justice system to light for the general public. This was very important volunteer work for me from 2009-2011.

Community Literacy Center: Established to create alternative literacy opportunities that work to educate and empower underserved populations. The Center supports university literacy research and outreach that promotes community action and social change.

literacy.colostate.edu/

It is through the CLC that I am able to write every Wednesday evening with the women of the Larimer County Detention Center.

John Barbato, artist

John stayed in Mexico with his writerly girlfriend, Beth. Please take a look at John's whoa-baby-it's-a-great-big-beautiful-crazy-world-out-there art at www.absolutearts.com/portfolio/j/johnbarbato. Great folk, great friends.

ABOUT THE AUTHOR

It's here in the book.

If you have additional questions or comments, please feel free to email me at ixcotel03@gmail.com

Or go to mesanger.wordpress.com/book to leave a message.

I look forward to hearing from you!

Made in the USA
Charleston, SC
29 March 2014